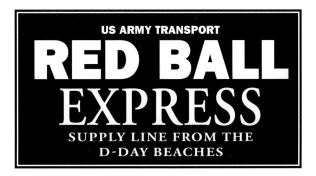

US ARMY TRANSPORT

RED BALL
EXPRESS

SUPPLY LINE FROM THE
D-DAY BEACHES

PAT WARE

Ian Allan
PUBLISHING

Acknowledgements

This book could not have been produced without the invaluable assistance of the following people: David Fletcher at the Tank Museum Bovington, England *(TM)*; Luther Hanson at the US Army Quartermasters Museum *(QM)*, Fort Lee, VA; Carolyn Wright at the US Army Museum of Transport *(MT)* Fort Eustis, VA; and Ian Carter at the Imperial War Museum for locating the US Embassy Collection *(IWM/USE)*. Also to David Doyle *(DD)* and Fred Crismon *(FC)* for additional material and to Phil Royal *(PR)*, Simon Thomson *(ST)*, John Blackman *(JB)* and Mark Barnes *(MB)* for their superb colour images. Finally to Martin Baldessari for his research at the US National Archives *(NA)* in Washington, DC.

Note: *All fluid measurements are given in US gallons and litres; weight measurements are given in long tons and tonnes.*

Pat Ware
Woolwich, London
July 2007

Conceived and edited by Jasper Spencer-Smith
Design editor: Nigel Pell
Colour and mono scanning: JPS Litho Ltd, Branksome, Dorset, BH12 1DJ
Produced by JSS Publishing Limited: PO Box 6031, Bournemouth, Dorset, BH1 9AT

First published 2007

ISBN (10) 0 7110 3192 4
ISBN (13) 978 0 7110 3192 0

Published by Ian Allan Publishing

An imprint of Ian Allan Publishing Ltd, Hersham, Surrey KT12 4RG

Printed by Ian Allan Printing Ltd, Hersham, Surrey KT12 4RG

Code 0709/C

Title spread: Fuel was the lifeblood of the invasion. Without adequate supplies there would be no advance. The lead vehicle is a White or Autocar tractor, coupled to a 2,000-gallon (7,600 litre) tanker semi-trailer. The vehicle following is the very similar Federal 94X43. *(NA)*

Contents

Introduction

Following the successful landings in Normandy, the Allies had planned that the advancing forces would be kept supplied by both rail and road, with overland pipelines carrying fuel. For a number of reasons this proved impossible and, in order to maintain the combat units as they pushed towards Germany, virtually all supplies were transported by road along designated supply routes.

Right: The immediate target for the Red Ball Express was to shift 102,000 tons (103,623 tonnes) of ammunition and various supplies, together with bulk petrol, oil and lubricants (POL), from forward dumps around the Normandy beachheads into a triangular area formed by the French towns of Chartres, Dreux and La Loupe. *(NA)*

The Red Ball Express was nothing more than the name given to a truck convoy system operating between St Lô and Paris between August and November 1944. It was hastily organised by two officers assigned to the headquarters of the US Army 'communications zone' (COMZ), the command responsible for lines of communication in the areas liberated by the advancing armies. Red Ball's role was to maintain supplies to the US Army during the hectic dash across France, which followed the Allied breakout from the Normandy beachheads. Once the Allies had the *Wehrmacht* retreating, the relative lack of resistance meant that ammunition supplies were never critical, but the speed at which Patton's Third Army and Hodge's First Army swept across France meant that the supply of adequate quantities of fuel and lubricants became crucial… and even threatened to halt the advance.

The Allies' original invasion plan had called for co-ordination between three methods of transport to supply the advancing armies - railways, roads and pipelines - but two things militated against this. Firstly, so much damage had been caused to the French railway system by the French resistance fighters and Allied bombings during the weeks preceding the D-Day landings that the use of the railways was out of the question. And secondly, the armies were advancing at such a speed that the use of pipelines, which could not be laid at more than 30 miles (48km) a day, was impractical.

By 22 August 1944, US forces had reached Sens, southeast of Paris, and it was clear that more and more road transport would be required to allow the advancing armies to stock their roadheads.

Clearly, road transport was the only viable option for delivering fuel, food, medical supplies, ammunition and oil in the quantities that were required.

On the night of 23 August 1944, the decision was taken to maximise the use of available road space by introducing a massive one-way loop highway between St Lô and the triangular area formed by the towns of Dreux, Chartres and La Loupe, with trucks driven around the clock.

One route was designated for outbound loaded trucks, with a different route for the unloaded inbound vehicles. No civilian traffic was permitted to use these roads.

The first Red Ball convoys - the name was derived from the use of 'red ball' as a railway slang term to indicate fast freight - began to roll on 25 August 1944, initially running for five days. The prime aim was to deliver 75,000 tons (76,363 tonnes) of supplies, plus huge quantities of bulk petrol, oil and lubricants (POL) into the Dreux triangle by the beginning of September. By 29 August, the end of the first phase, 132 US Army truck companies were involved, and almost 6,000 trucks delivered 12,342 tons (12,566 tonnes) of supplies on that one day.

The first phase of the operation was subsequently extended until 4 September, by which time 89,939 tons (91,378 tonnes) of supplies had been delivered, at a cost of 300,000 (US) gallons (1,140,000 litres) of petrol a day.

Eisenhower's decision to allow Patton's Third US Army to pursue the *Wehrmacht* across the Seine meant that the Red Ball operation could not be terminated, and a second phase of the operation immediately followed. The faster Patton advanced, the more extended the lines of supply became. Now there were daily targets, the average being 4,552 tons (4,625,060kg). The operation was continued until 16 November 1944. By this time, the route was extended eastwards as far as Soissons and Sommesous… and the average round trip was more than 600 miles (1000km).

The total tonnage delivered in phase two exceeded 323,000 (328,872 tonnes).

More than 5,900 trucks operated by 133 'light' and 'heavy' truck companies were involved at the peak of the operation. Vehicles used included 2½-ton, 6x6 trucks, sometimes with 1-ton trailers.

Also used were 1½-ton and 4-5-ton 4x2 vehicles, 4x4 tractor/semi-trailer outfits and even tank transporter tractors. Jeeps and motorcycles were used by the US Military Police to keep the supply routes open. US Army truck recovery companies operated medium and heavy wreckers. The majority (75%) of the personnel operating the Red Ball trucks were African-American troops, even though these men formed less than 10% of the strength of the US Army.

At the height of the operation, Patton's Third Army alone was consuming close to 1,000,000 gallons (3,800,000 litres) of fuel a day. The speed of the advance was such that there were times when Red Ball trucks could not keep up and it was necessary for fuel to be delivered to forward areas by aircraft to allow the operation to continue.

When the operation had begun, the hope had always been that Patton would be able to secure a rapid 'knock-out' punch against the *Wehrmacht* and nobody anticipated that the Red Ball operation would last so long. Although the strain on personnel and equipment was considerable, with accidents becoming commonplace through a combination of fatigue, overloading and mechanical breakdown, at no time was the US Army's advance slowed by a lack of fuel.

To this day, many believe that all US Army convoy operations in the European Theatre were referred to as the Red Ball Express. This is not the case; as the service operated for just 81 days but it was the first, the longest and perhaps the most ambitious of US Army supply operations. There were also several other 'express' transportation projects, including the so-

called 'Red Lion' or 'BB' route running from Bayeux to Brussels carrying supplies for Montgomery's ill-fated 'Operation Market Garden' when 1,400 British Army trucks were out of action with engine problems due to the introduction of leaded fuel. Other routes included the Green Diamond Express, the White Ball Express, the Little Red Ball and the so-called ABC and XYZ operations – the latter carrying the largest tonnage of supplies and also being the most efficient.

Although there was little glory attached to the hard-working men operating the Red Ball Express, there can be no doubt that the operation maintained the very lifeblood flowing through the arteries of World War Two. Without the Red Ball Express, the war in Europe would possibly have dragged on for many more months.

Above: A Jeep stands at the head of a convoy of 2¹/₂-ton GMC trucks waiting to slip in behind the moving lines of vehicles. Jeeps, Dodge and GMCs were frequently employed as lead vehicles for the massive convoys which rolled across north-west France. *(IWM/USE)*

1 | A Logistics Nightmare

The Red Ball Express was the first of a series of special truck convoys. It operated on public roads which were closed to other traffic, using a massive one way system between St Lô and Paris during the period August to November 1944. Red Ball's role was to carry food, fuel, ammunition, lubricants and ordnance supplies to the advancing units of the US First and Third Armies.

Right: A GMC tractor unit decorated by the driver with .50in calibre cartridges and a pin-up in the cab windscreen *(NA)*

The lack of fuel and ammunition almost forced the US Armies to halt their advance across France. During World War Two, the movement of men and, more particularly, supplies en masse over great distances, became one of the most vital military interests to the Allies. Effective transportation was vital in bringing the power of the Allied armies to bear successfully against the enemy. Nowhere was this more evident than in Normandy in the months following the D-Day landings, and supply logistics became crucial to the success of Operation Overlord.

It was calculated that the invasion and follow-on forces would require 16,000,000 tons (16,256,000 tonnes) of supplies, 4,200 tanks and other tracked vehicles, 3,500 artillery pieces, 140,000 transport vehicles and 12,000 aircraft. By D+20 (26 June 1944) it was assumed that the Allied supply lines would be able to deliver 5,000 tons (5,080 tonnes) per day of petrol, oil and lubricants (POL), rising to 10,000 tons (10,160 tonnes) per day by D+90.

Petrol weighs approximately 7.7lb (3.49kg) per gallon, so this equates to 1,500,000 gallons (6,819,000 litres) a day by D+20 and 3,000,000 gallons (13,638,000 litres) a day by D+90! Some of this fuel was to be pumped ashore from tankers, with subsequent onward shipping by pipeline, road or rail. Great reliance was also placed on PLUTO (pipeline under the ocean) – the project to deliver massive quantities of fuel that were required. Connection to the French coast did not happen until the surrender of German forces in Cherbourg on 27 June 1944, and then pumping did not begin until 12 August 1944.

Although trucks were considered to be crucial in delivering supplies to the combat troops, the planners had assumed that trucks would not be used for hauling supplies over distances greater than 150 miles (245km). What was not known at the time these plans were being prepared was that the French railway system would be out of action for months following D-Day due to the success of pre-invasion

Above: During World War Two, the United States became known as the 'arsenal of democracy'. Between 1939 and 1945, the US motor industry produced more than 3,000,000 transport vehicles, 88,000 tanks, and 41,000 half-tracks. In the weeks following D-Day, thousands of these vehicles were shipped across to Normandy. (MT)

air attacks and sabotage activities. The failure to capture the port of Cherbourg intact meant that supplies would continue to be delivered from the D-Day beachheads for many weeks following the landings.

Combined with other factors, these miscalculations could ultimately have led to the failure of Operation Overlord as the supply lines became more and more extended from the beachhead.

Planning for Overlord

US Army Major-General Frank Ross was the man responsible for all aspects of transportation, including road, rail, water and air, in the all-important European Theatre of Operation.

Transportation for line of supply falls under the jurisdiction of what was known

as the communications zone (COMZ), the area immediately to the rear of the combat zone of a theatre of war which contains the lines of communications and establishments for supply and evacuation. Also other agencies required for the immediate support and maintenance of the field forces. Prior to the autumn of 1943, the US Army's transportation planning for Operation Overlord had been allocated to a small section under the command of Colonel David W. Traub, who subsequently went on to become Deputy Chief of Transportation.

In the absence of firm operational plans, which were still being prepared, supply requirements were projected on the basis of anticipated troop strengths. Detailed planning was not able to begin until October 1943 when the plan for

Overlord began to be distributed. The Motor Transport Division assumed the use of standard truck companies, each equipped with 40 standardised $2^1/_2$-ton 6x6 trucks, which would be overloaded by 100% to carry a 5-ton (5,080kg) load. With a single driver, the maximum average daily range was 50 miles (80km), which meant that each truck company would have a capacity of 10,000 ton/miles per day. By simple calculation, it was proposed that 240 truck companies would be required to meet the needs of port clearance, inter-depot and long-distance line of communication movement. Unwilling to accept this figure, 'theatre headquarters' attempted to reduce the number of truck companies to 100 and grudgingly settled on a final figure of 160.

Having observed British experiences in North Africa, Ross proposed re-equipping a large proportion of the truck companies with larger vehicles. In August 1943, he told Washington that the 160 companies should be made up of two heavy truck companies to every one light truck company. Only the latter, comprising 61 companies, were to be equipped with $2^1/_2$ ton 6x6 GMCs and, of these, 36 were to be issued with AFKWX forward-control trucks. These allowed a greater payload to be carried due to longer cargo-carrying beds; an additional 27 companies were to be issued with 750-gallon (2,850 litres) GMC fuel tankers. Two companies were to be equipped with 5-ton refrigerated semi-trailers for food deliveries, 59 companies with 4 to 5 ton tractors hauling 10-ton (gross weight) semi-trailers, and nine

Above: A $2^1/_2$-ton GMC 6x6, loaded with tyres, pulls away whilst a 5-ton International tractor waits to be loaded by a Thew crane. *(TM)*

Above: Another loaded convoy moves out. In each case the lead vehicle is a Jeep, and whilst most of the trucks are the ubiquitous 2½-ton GMC, the convoy on the left consists of 5-ton International tractors with semi-trailers. *(NA)*

companies with 2,000-gallon (7,600 litres) semi-trailer fuel tankers. Finally, two companies were to be issued with Diamond T M19 tank-transporter tractors and draw-bar trailers which had been converted for carrying over-sized and dense cargo.

Approval of the revised plan did not come until December 1943 by which time difficulties with the manufacture and supply of trucks in sufficient volume meant that it was doubtful whether even the scaled-down programme would be met. By March 1944, just three months before the launch of the D-Day invasion, only 66 10-ton semi-trailers had been supplied against a requirement of 7,194, and none of the tractor units had been delivered.

The Transportation Corps was increasingly fearful that serious delays in motor transport would hamper the entire Overlord operation.

In April 1944, the Chief of Transportation shared these fears with the High Command in Washington, pointing out that he would require all of the requested vehicles in order to fulfil the stated mission. It seems that there was no real agreement between the authorities and, in any case, it was too late for the requested vehicles to be made available. In a last ditch attempt to shore up the transportation situation, various substitute trucks were ordered to be released by the US Army ground forces, Army Air Force and Army service forces.

Thus, the Transportation Corps was equipped with several hundred Chevrolet 1½-ton tractor units designed for use with a 6-ton gross weight semi-trailer; these had originally been developed for use in southeast Asia. In addition, there were 4 to 5 ton tractors with recovery-type semi-trailers as well as other miscellaneous, and not necessarily suitable, types. It was promised that 1,750 new 4 to 5 ton tractor units and 3,500 10-ton semi-trailers would be diverted from Burma where they had been positioned for use in the construction of the Ledo Road.

As D-Day approached, Ross believed that the plan for the deployment of motor transport was the least satisfactory of the transport functions,

and his 'heavy vehicle' conversion project did not get underway until almost six months after the D-Day landings. However, by means of the last minute round-up of, occasionally unsuitable, vehicles, Washington (aka the US government) hoped to ride through the critical period. The only piece of good news was that Washington had finally agreed that 100% overloading of the trucks was acceptable providing they were 'operated on smooth, hard-surfaced roads'.

But, as D-Day loomed ever closer, Transportation Corps personnel were nervous that there would be serious shortages in cargo-carrying capacity, from perhaps as early as D+30. These same personnel were later to express the opinion that the lack of suitable vehicles contributed to the slowness of combat operations in the first few days of September.

As if this was not bad enough, there was also a shortage of manpower.

Ross had also learned from British operations in North Africa that there was considerable value in having sufficient drivers to operate around the clock. As early as August 1943, Transportation Corps officials had requested 36 additional drivers per truck company, which would be sufficient to provide two drivers per vehicle. The request was denied. Ross was convinced that 24-hour working would be essential to the success of the operation. Under pressure, General Lee, Commander of Services of Supply, European Theatre of Operations, USA (known by the acronym 'SOS ETOUSA'), finally agreed to transfer 5,600 men from other units in order to increase the number of drivers in the 140 truck companies. Sadly, many of these men were poorly trained and were unsuitable for the new role; many had never even driven a truck before.

The transportation plan was finally incorporated into the Forward Echelon, Communications Zone (FECZ) plan issued in May 1944.

It was envisaged that during the first 40 days following D-Day, US lines of communication would be extended in a north-south direction along an axis passing through Cherbourg and Vitré. Men and supplies would be discharged over the beaches and through the minor ports on the Cotentin Peninsular and would flow, either southwards to depots, or direct to battlefront units. All logistical operations at this stage were to be controlled by the US First Army with personnel supplied from the attached Advance Section, Communications Zone

(ASCZ). Some transport personnel landed in France as early as D+1.

As the combat troops moved forward, the Advance Section (ADSEC) would gradually take responsibility for activities in the communications zone and around D+20, a rear boundary would be drawn behind the First Army. By D+41, it was anticipated that the lines of communication would become oriented more to an east-west direction, with supplies coming through ports in northern Brittany and flowing in the direction of Brest-Le Mans, with a base depot established to handle these supplies. At that time, the plan assumed that there would be 130 truck companies deployed in France and ADSEC would start to move forward in support of advancing combat troops.

As it happened, nothing worked out as planned and various factors combined to jeopardise combat operations.

The campaign for Normandy

At the end of D-Day, 6 June 1944, the Allies had landed more than 130,000 troops on the five Normandy beaches, gaining a foothold in Hitler's Fortress Europe.

Forward elements of ADSEC started to land from as early as D+1, and were attached to the US First Army to assist in operating the beachheads until ADSEC and COMZ were in a position to assume control. The ADSEC Motor Transport Brigade landed in increments commencing on D+3.

During the following weeks, Allied air superiority, together with a reluctance on the part of the *Wehrmacht* to move troops from elsewhere, allowed the Allied build-up to continue. But the Germans recovered quickly and, although the Allies managed to push some

20 miles (32km) or so inland, by the beginning of July the front was at a virtual stalemate.

By this time there were more than 800,000 Allied soldiers in France, and some 148,803 vehicles had been landed, together with 570,505 tons (579,633 tonnes) of supplies. The lack of significant forward progress meant that the rear areas were becoming crowded, with supplies frequently stacked in the open, often in the middle of fields with little camouflage from air attack. Towards the end of July, the rear areas in Normandy had progressed as far as possible, except for the reconstruction of ports, which was seriously hampering the offloading of most supplies. The weather in July had been unseasonably

poor, and this also contributed to the local difficulties.

Discharge from the beaches and small ports had been developed to maximum capacity, with upwards of 30,000 tons (30,480 tonnes) being cleared by road every day. Advance Section had taken over all US Army installations in the area with the exception of POL dumps. Supplies were being stored as far forward as was feasible in the areas of Omaha Beach and the town of St Lô. Even though only 94 of the planned 130 truck companies were in operation under ADSEC, the supply situation was considered to be 'good' albeit there were shortages of certain types of clothing and weapons (Class II supplies, see panel) and ammunition (Class V). Neither the

Above: Whilst by no means the only truck used on the supply routes, with more than 500,000 produced between 1941 and 1944, the GMC 6x6 was the mainstay of the supply routes. Note the rack behind the cab carrying 12 Jerrycans, equivalent to 52 (US) gallons (240 litres) of petrol. *(IWM/USE)*

Above: A Plymouth P11 sedan leads this Red Ball re-enactment. *(PR)*

First nor Third Armies were maintaining anything like the authorised 'seven units of fire', in other words, days of available ammunition. The Communications Zone held nine days supply of general ammunition, 11.1 days supply of artillery ammunition and 16 days supply of POL. On the plus side, there was no shortage of rations.

Brigadier General Ewart G. Plank of the Advance Section believed that the armies could continue to be supplied 'without any difficulties'.

It was not until 25 July that 'Operation Cobra' was launched when the US First and Third Armies broke out of the Cotentin Peninsular. Seizing the bridge over the Sélune river at Pontaubault, south of Avranches on 31 July, General Omar Bradley's First US Army had potentially opened the routes west into Brittany, south towards the Loire, and east into Paris. However, despite Bradley's successes

at Pontaubault, the Germans continued to hold firm elsewhere. The major port of Brest was not captured until 19 September 1944 and the port and submarine base of Lorient remained under German control until May 1945.

In late July, Bradley handed command of the First US Army to General Courtney H. Hodges.

At the beginning of August 1944, ADSEC assumed control of what had previously been the Normandy Base Section and established a headquarters in Valognes, between Cherbourg and Carentan. The delivery of supplies during the first weeks of August continued to be substantial.

On 8 August, Hodges' US First Army together with General George S. Patton Jr's US Third Army, and with help from the Canadians, encircled 21 German divisions west of Argenten and Falaise. Three days later, as Hodges and Patton

moved to trap the fleeing Germans, the daily POL requirement for Advance Section had been doubled from 300,000 gallons (1,140,000 litres) to 600,000 gallons (2,280,000 litres). Bradley, now commanding the 12th Army Group, which ultimately comprised the US First, Third, Ninth and 12th Armies, temporarily halted the operation for reasons which remain unexplained. Nevertheless, by 18 August, thousands of Germans were effectively trapped in the Falaise pocket and, in attempting to escape through a narrow gap, they lost between 25,000 and 50,000 men while sustaining hundreds of thousands of casualties. Huge quantities of weapons, equipment and vehicles were abandoned or destroyed.

With the attack moving once again, Patton followed in hot pursuit. On 19 August, General Dwight D. Eisenhower, Supreme Commander of Operation Overlord, allowed Patton, Bradley and the British General Bernard Montgomery to cross the Seine. The Germans were clearly in full-scale retreat and Eisenhower resolved that the Allies would strike immediately for the German border, believing that it might be possible to destroy the *Wehrmacht* in France. This would effectively end the war in Europe before the onset of winter 1944/45. On 21 August, Eisenhower announced that he would take personal control of the Allied ground forces from 1 September. He informed Bradley that his 12th Army Group was to advance to the French-German border, whilst Montgomery's 21st Army Group, made up of the Second British and First Canadian Armies, was to advance into Belgium through the Nord and Pas de Calais regions.

As Patton pressed further eastward towards Germany, the Third Army's quartermasters were struggling to keep forward units adequately fuelled and maintained. The doubling of the daily fuel

Above: Maintenance was initially carried out on the '40+8' system, meaning that for every 40 trucks operating, eight would be undergoing servicing by unit mechanics. *(JB)*

allowance was already proving to be insufficient and, by this time, the average consumption stood at 800,000 gallons (3,040,000 litres) a day. On 24 August, Hodge's First Army alone had consumed 782,000 gallons (2,971,600 litres) which was more than the daily allowance for both armies.

By 29 August, Patton had reached the Marne and, just six days into battle, the Third Army daily combat diary records that 'supply lines were lengthening rapidly and putting a strain on the truck companies'. There was little choice but to start using emergency ration reserves and 'liberating' available stocks of fuel from other units. So rapid was the advance that items as diverse as communication wire and medical supplies were in equally short supply.

Patton's quartermasters requested additional truck and aircraft companies to improve medical evacuation and resupply efforts. In late August, over 1,000 aircraft delivered rations and fuel to Patton's forward elements. This avoided the necessity for a complete halt to the advance for a few more days. At the same time captured German supplies, including food, medical supplies, POL, and communications wire, were utilised.

As the German forces crossed the Seine and streamed across north-east France towards Belgium, Luxembourg and the Homeland, Patton followed, crossing the Seine at Melun and Fontainebleau on D+79... some 11 days ahead of the date predicted in the Overlord plan. It had originally been intended that the Allies would halt at the Seine. This would allow

Above: Major Jerry House (left) of the Maintenance Division, Motor Transport Brigade, ASCZ, discusses the route with Colonel Richmond commanding officer of the Motor Transport Brigade, whilst Captain Arthur Chester, Chief of Military and Civilian Personnel looks on. *(PW)*

Far left: 1½-ton Chevrolet 4x4 tractor (G4100/G7100 series) with the 3½-6 ton stake and platform semi-trailer. These trailers were produced by a variety of manufacturers including Winter-Weiss, Black Diamond, Hobbs and Strick. They were intended specifically for use with the Chevrolet tractor. *(NA)*

Both pages: Fuel was the lifeblood of the supply routes. Some two weeks after D-Day, motor fuel and aviation spirit were being pumped ashore at Port-en-Bessin from tankers. Steel pipelines were laid alongside the D6 road, carrying the fuel from Port-en-Bessin to the US fuel tank farm at Mont Cauvin. By D+21 there were 7,500,000 tons (7,620,000 tonnes) of fuel and other petroleum products in Normandy. Jerrycans were a vital component in the fuel supply system but thousands were discarded along the supply routes eventually leading to a shortage. *(MB)*

time for a depot and supply base system to be consolidated, which could support the troops as the advance continued across France towards Germany. The depots were intended to be sited between the French cities of Rennes and Laval.

However, there was to be no respite. Patton continued the advance, consuming petrol at an incredible rate as well as requiring ammunition, food and other vital supplies, all of which were continuing to come from Normandy, more than 200 miles (322km) away. The faster Patton's army advanced, the more fuel was consumed in simply trying to maintain supplies. The supply situation rapidly became critical. The difficulties of moving fuel, ammunition and other matériel to the battlefront effectively curtailed further combat operations.

At the beginning of August, the armies had been required to maintain seven days supply of rations, POL and ammunition. By 27 August, the figure had been reduced to five days. Even this stock level was hopelessly optimistic since 95% of the US Army's supplies still lay in the base depots in the vicinity of the beaches.

Few on the Allied side had anticipated how rapidly the speed of the advance would precipitate a supply crisis by the end of August deliveries to combat units began to significantly fall short.

With the Third Army rapidly approaching the German frontier, COMZ struggled to keep the Allied forces

supplied. Not only were there a continuing shortage of trucks and misplaced allocation priorities, but there were more troops in the communications zone than had ever been intended.

On 27 August, Bradley stated that 'the armies will go as far as practicable and then wait until the supply system in rear will permit further advance'. Within days of this announcement, Patton was at Troyes, having captured intact the bridges at Verdun and Commercy. However, his allocation of fuel had been cut by 90% in favour of Hodges and Montgomery. His tanks had now effectively run out of fuel.

Whilst Napoléon Bonaparte, that great French tactician, may have believed that an 'army marched on its stomach', by 1944, the US Army rarely marched into battle. True, the men needed to be fed, but it was possible for them to consume local produce and to eat captured enemy supplies. What they needed above all else was fuel. Without fuel, the Third Army's advance halted.

The Germans described the result of this situation as the 'miracle in the West'. But to the US forces it was nothing less than a catastrophe.

A massive supply crisis had been precipitated by the rapid breakout from Normandy and it was clear that it had become impossible to supply the advancing armies at the necessary scale.

The US First Army was estimating its daily average tonnage requirement at 5,500 tons (5,588 tonnes), including 2,200

Left: The PLUTO (pipeline under the ocean) project was intended to provide fuel to the advancing Allied armies after D-Day. The pipelines came ashore at Cherbourg and Port en Bessin in Normandy, also later in the Pas de Calais region. On land, the fuel was pumped through steel pipes laid alongside the roads. *(PW)*

US Army supplies categories

Class I: supplies which are consumed at a predictable rate such as rations
Class II: clothing and weapons
Class III: petrol, lubricating oils, grease and other petroleum products
Class IV: miscellaneous supplies, including construction materials
Class V: ammunition, explosives and chemical weapons

tons (2,235 tonnes) of POL and 1,100 tons (1,118 tonnes) of ammunition. Patton's Third Army requested a daily figure of 6,000 tons (6,096 tonnes), including 1,411 tons (1,434 tonnes) of POL and 2,545 tons (2,586 tonnes) of ammunition. In addition, Patton wanted a further 12,500 tons (12,700 tonnes) of clothing, weapons and construction materials plus a further 15,000 tons (15,240 tonnes) of ammunition to help build up reserves.

The delivery of a total of 39,000 tons (39,624 tonnes) of supplies per day was out of the question. Not because the supplies were unavailable, but because they were located at the Normandy beachhead and there was simply no suitable transportation available to get the supplies to the army dumps – which by this time were some 300 miles (483km) away. The situation deteriorated to the point where just the barest essentials were being delivered, on a day-to-day basis. Such forward supply depots as existed moved at the same rapid pace as the combat troops. Drivers bringing truckloads of much-needed supplies from the Normandy area frequently found that the depots had been moved and were required to travel a further 20 to 30 miles (32 to 48km). This at

the scheduled rate of 50 miles (80.5km) a day, could often take up to another six or seven hours to achieve. And the drivers often found themselves literally at the front-line, either waiting for pockets of enemy troops to be cleared, or fighting their way to a rendezvous.

Troops of the US First and Third Armies could continue to move forward without food since they were able to live off the countryside, and the lack of opposition meant that the expenditure of ammunition was lower than predicted. But it was impossible for the advance to

continue without fuel. Patton summed up the situation admirably in a conversation with Eisenhower on 2 September 1944: 'My men can eat their belts, but my tanks gotta have gas.'

The logistics at COMZ, by now based in Paris, despaired of developing effective lines of communication and supply which could match the speed of advance. Despite having issued 550 additional GMC 2¹/₂-ton trucks and borrowed more than 350 3 and 6 ton-class trucks from the British 21st Army Group for a whole month, it was

only possible to support the forward units at what was described as an 'adequate scale'.

Faced with shortages of trucks and men, consumption of fuel at levels which had not been predicted, and ever-lengthening lines of communication, it was obvious that a more effective method of marshalling the existing (and scarcely adequate) transportation resources was the solution.

COMZ's eventual solution to the problem of expediting delivery of supplies was the Red Ball Express.

Above: Supply dump and convoy viewed from the air. After D-Day, forward dumps like these were established around the bridgehead area. *(NA)*

2 Necessity is the Mother of Invention

By the end of August 1944, 28 US Army Divisions were advancing across France and Belgium, each requiring 700-750 tons of supplies a day. The total daily requirement was in the order of 20,000 tons and, although there was no shortage of supplies in France, the real problems lay in getting these supplies from the Normandy beachheads to the advancing armies.

Right: Although far less common, the forward-control GMC AFKWX was also an important component in the operation of the supply routes. The extended truck bed actually allowed some operational advantage. It was first produced in 1942 and remained in production throughout the war. *(TM)*

At the end of August 1944, the US First and Third Armies were continuing to pursue the fleeing German Army to the point where the US lines of communication were stretched to the limit; what had been a 50-mile (80km) line on 1 August had become 400 miles (644km) by 1 September. Some 28 Divisions were advancing across France and Belgium, each requiring 700 to 750 tons (711,235-762,037kg) of supplies a day, giving a total daily consumption of 20,000 tons (20,320 tonnes).

Following the breakout, the First and Third Armies were in desperate need of fuel, ammunition and other supplies. Each combat division had its own truck companies which could transport matériel from the forward dumps and depots to the front line. However the problems lay further back in the supply chain, and there were difficulties in actually getting the supplies from the Normandy beachheads to the advancing armies.

It was logistical factors, rather than combat operations, which were conspiring to hold back the Allied advance towards Germany. Faced with a shortfall of transport rather than supplies, head-quarters' staff in the Communications Zone (COMZ-HQ) were faced with having to devise a way to push forward supplies of all types to a new base from which the advancing armies could draw what was required. At the same time, large numbers of trucks were being used to haul equipment for the construction of fuel pipelines and depots which led to a shortage of trucks and personnel.

Clearly, the urgency of the requirement called for drastic measures. Yet this same urgency also meant that little time was available for planning, and certainly, there was no time available for trials. Advance Section (ADSEC) had already attempted to offset the shortage of trucks by pooling some 90 ADSEC quartermaster truck companies into a single organisation known as the Advance Section Motor Transport Brigade (ASMTB), initially under the command of Colonel Clarence W. Richmond.

Above: Standard 40-gallon (182 litre) drums were used to transport lubricating oils. *(QM)*

Right: Literally millions of Jerrycans were used throught the operation. At one time, a shortage of cans forced the military authorities to offer civilians a bounty for returning discarded cans to supply depots. *(IWM/USE)*

And yet the shortage of trucks persisted. Clearly, if no extra trucks could be found, then some way had to be devised to use the existing trucks in a way that was both more efficient and productive.

The solution was the Red Ball Express, an emergency transportation plan which employed every available truck company, working around the clock, on roads which were cleared of all other traffic. The decision to establish the operation was made by Brigadier-General Ewart G. Plank of ADSEC during a 36-hour brainstorming session which ended on the night of 23 August 1944. Stung by criticisms of the existing transport operation, Plank apparently prefaced his decision with the words 'let it never be said that ADSEC stopped Patton when the Germans couldn't'.

In essence, the Red Ball operation was simple – all units performing trucking tasks behind ADSEC were to be used to move ordnance and petrol to the combat troops as fast as possible.

The practical details of the operation were thrashed out by Lieutenant-Colonel Loren A. Ayers and Major Gordon K. Gravelle, both of the COMZ headquarters' staff. In June, the MTB had joined ADSEC HQ as part of a Motor Transport Division but the division was now redesignated as COMZ Motor Transport Service, under the command of Lieutenant-Colonel Ayers.

The Red Ball Express began 36 hours after the decision was taken.

The name 'Red Ball Express' was borrowed from rail freight operations where it simply meant fast through freight. It was not a new idea. The Transportation Corps had already briefly experimented with a similar trial run for moving supplies from the dumps in Great Britain to the Channel shipping ports. What was new, was the idea that the operation would run continuously, 24 hours a day. However it

Above: Before the establishment of working harbours, supplies were unloaded directly onto the beaches and then moved inland to supply dumps. *(MT)*

soon became obvious that the trial had hardly served as an adequate test for the problems which were to arise during continuous, large-scale operations.

Ayers and Gravelle assigned all but five of the motor transport companies available in the Communications Zone, some 141 truck companies, to newly-formed COMZ sections for 'line of communication' transport. Ten additional

trucks were issued to each of 55 companies and 40 truck units were re-assigned from base sections to the ASMTB. The remaining five companies were used for railhead work.

Most of the trucks employed were of the standardised $2^{1}/_{2}$-ton 6x6 GMC type, either the bonneted CCKW, the famous 'Jimmy' - or the forward-control AFKWX with both types occasionally towing 1-ton

two-wheeled Ben-Hur trailers. Other trucks included Chevrolet 1^1/$_2$-ton tractors, Studebaker 2^1/$_2$-ton tractors, and 4 to 5 ton Autocar, Federal, International, Kenworth and Marmon-Herrington tractors, all intended for use with various types of semi-trailer.

At some stage in the operation, (possibly in mid-August but the official sources appear to differ as to when this actually happened) two companies were equipped with Diamond T M19 tank-transporter tractors and draw-bar trailers which had been converted for carrying over-sized loads; these were used to carry massive amounts of ammunition, Jerrycans of 'packaged' POL or other 'dense' loads.

Convoy commanders travelled by Jeep or, occasionally by Dodge command car.

Above: White, Mack, Brockway and Corbitt all produced 6-ton 6x6 chassis which were equipped for a variety of roles. This example mounts a Quick-Way turntable crane which is being used to load supplies. *(NA)*

Right: A GMC 6x6 being loaded by crews using the same type of crane. *(NA)*

Finally, although the Allies had virtual control of the skies over Normandy, numbers of the convoy vehicles were fitted with machine gun mounts. At times Dodge 6x6 trucks equipped with .30 and .50 calibre machine guns in 'quad' mounts were assigned to the convoys for air defence.

By 1 September, the immediate target was to shift 102,000 tons (103,632 tonnes) of various supplies, together with bulk petrol, oil and lubricants, from the forward dumps around the beachheads into a triangular area formed by the French towns of Chartres, Dreux and La Loupe. It was assumed that 20,000 tons (20,320 tonnes) would be delivered by rail, leaving the remainder to be carried by road on a one-way loop road system. This was a system of parallel road routes running eastwards from St Lô through Vire and Alençon to Chartres on the outward journey. The vehicles then returned empty on a more southerly loop

west, which passed through Nogent-le-Rotrou, Mayenne and Mortain.

The route was planned to run on many minor 'departmental' roads, passing through the centres of many small towns and villages. Even today, some 60 years later, it is not difficult to imagine what these roads must have been like when jammed with military traffic. The need to keep the routes clear for the Red Ball Express was considered so important that a message to this effect was printed in several Parisian newspapers during the closing days of September as well as being broadcast on the BBC French Service and several European radio stations. Read by General Lee, the message stated…

'Today one of our most important weapons of war is the Red Ball Highway. Winding in and out of tiny towns and hamlets, sometimes even cutting through the heart of big cities, this great network of roads links the ports and beaches with our fighting fronts. Everywhere it can be easily

Above: The lack of significant forward progress following the establishment of a foothold on French soil meant that the rear areas were becoming crowded with supplies. These were frequently stacked in the open, often in the middle of fields with little camouflage from air attack. *(NA)*

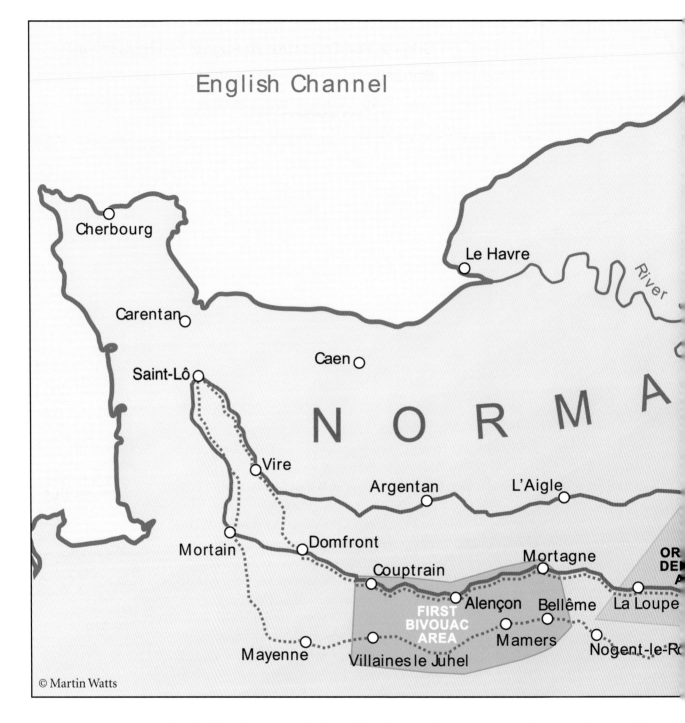

© Martin Watts

identified by the signs of the Red Ball. They mean (the route is) reserved for high-speed, non-stop military traffic only. In order to get the greatest efficiency from our system of land convoys, the traffic on these roads goes one way only.

At the front, soldiers are waiting for guns and gasoline, bombs and bullets, and many other military essentials. The Red

Ball convoys carry these supplies over the Red Ball Highway. That's why they've got to go through fast – not tomorrow – but right now. Thousands of lives may be sacrificed by a few seconds of needless delay. A thoughtless civilian driving a slow touring car can hold up a whole convoy – priceless time lost, priceless lives too. A two and a half ton truck has to swerve to

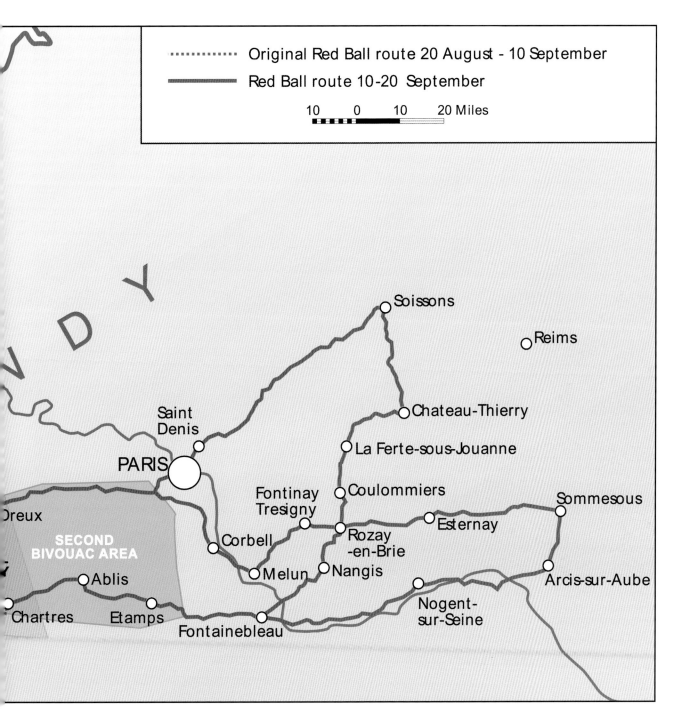

avoid hitting a cyclist – more time lost, more lives too.

Thus, in fairness to our fighting forces, we ask the civilian population not to interfere in any manner whatsoever with the free flow of military traffic which rushes over these roads night and day. We know you may be inconvenienced by taking small roads, or getting some place in a roundabout way, but the winning of the war must come before anything else. We know we can expect the full co-operation of the civilian population. Our supplies must get through… and on time.'

Military Police (MPs) were deployed as traffic controllers on the road. The route was clearly marked 'Red Ball Trucks Only' and MPs were empowered to turn back all

Above: By 1 September 1944, the first phase of the Red Ball operation was supposed to have been completed. The destruction of the French railway system by Allied bombing and sabotage by the Resistance meant that the system failed to cope with the assigned volume and virtually all of the supplies were moved by road. *(NA)*

civilian traffic; other military traffic was only permitted with prior permission from Advance Section (ADSEC); even ADSEC tank-transporter convoys were forced to take alternative routes.

The route

It is apparent that the complete route was not decided upon in detail until the afternoon of 27 August, and it was the restricted width of the roads in Normandy that led Richmond and Ayers to demand that a one-way working system be implemented.

Examining a map of present day France, it appears that the outbound route followed what is now the N174 from St Lô to Vire, continuing on the D924 to

Tinchebray, turning south on the D22 to Domfront, N176 to Pré-en-Pail, N12 to Alençon and Mortagne-au-Perche, before taking the D10 and D920 to La Loupe, and then finally east to Chartres on the N23 from Courville.

The return journey was slightly more direct, taking the D921 and D922 from Chartres towards Nogent-le-Rotrou, the D955 to Bellême and Mamers, D311 and D310 to Fresnay, D15 to Villaines-la-Juhel, D113 to Mayenne, and then the N12, D35 and D32 to Mortain, before crossing the outbound route on the N174 at Vire and then turning northeast on the D52 and D28 back to St Lô.

Some trucks were also required to travel north to the Normandy Base Section depot in the beachhead area, and

even to Cherbourg, to collect cargo. But the control point was established at St Lô, and it was here that the convoys were to be assembled and despatched after loading. COMZ-HQ Section G-4 supplied a daily list to Normandy Base Section showing the total tonnage to be transported, broken down by service, supply class and final destination. Daily logs were prepared at St Lô showing how these figures had been met. The daily logs were delivered to ADSEC by courier and transmitted twice daily by teletype (telex) to the relevant regulating stations.

Red Ball Express - Phase One

Initially 118 truck companies - although official documents mysteriously state that the figure was $117^2/_3$ companies, the $^2/_3$ coming from COMZ headquarters - were allocated to the Red Ball Express, with five reserved for railhead distribution in the Chartres-Le Mans area. More than 70 truck companies were already working under the control of ADSEC, 41 were to be supplied by motor transport of the Normandy Base Section and three from the Loire Section. Two British transport companies from the 21st Army Group, one equipped with 3 ton and one with 6 ton trucks, had been loaned to the US Army on 6 August, initially for an agreed period of eight days. The vehicles were also absorbed into the Red Ball operation, not being released until 4 September when the British Army's transport crisis was reaching a peak.

Above: Fuel was always a problem and Patton's advance was frequently slowed by its unavailability. These 4-5 ton tractors (Autocar or White) are towing 2,000-gallon (7,600 litre) semi-trailers and have another 2,000 gallons (7,600 litre) in a full trailer behind. Note the MP traffic controller. *(DD)*

The division of responsibility for the convoys was arranged on a geographical basis. ADSEC controlled all convoys, loaded or empty, which were east of St Lô. It was also tasked with getting empty trucks to the loading points, loading and ensuring that the vehicles were returned to the control point at St Lô when empty. Accommodation and truck-servicing points were set up at each of two administrative points.

The convoy destinations were the regulating stations of the US Armies to which the supplies were assigned. Each of these stations designated the dump to which the supplies were to be delivered, and arranged for the supplies to be offloaded at the appropriate time. The regulating stations were supposedly notified six or seven hours in advance of the arrival of the supplies which allowed arrangements to be made for prompt unloading to reduce turnaround time to the minimum. In practice this did not always happen and sometimes supplies arrived for unloading before the depot had received notice of the shipment being sent. This led to delays.

Starting with 67, out of the total 118 companies equipped with 3,358 trucks, mainly standardised GMC 2^{1}/$_{2}$-ton 6x6 vehicles, the operation began on 25 August 1944. By the end of the first day, 4,482 tons (4,553 tonnes) had been delivered to the Dreux-Chartres area. By 29 August, there were 132 companies at work with a (potential) fleet of 5,958 vehicles.

On that day, a record 12,342 tons (12,539 tonnes) of supplies were shifted.

Each convoy was fully loaded in accordance with the lists supplied by COMZ headquarters; any supplies that could not been loaded were backlogged and placed on the next day's list. Any backlogged items that had not been cleared within three days were considered for cancellation. Conversely, if there was more transport available than was called for to move the listed supplies, together with any backlog, then the surplus space was taken by POL and Class I supplies in equal quantities.

The trucks always moved in complete company unit convoys of approximately 40 vehicles; a company's full strength was 48 vehicles but 40 was a realistic figure allowing for maintenance and breakdowns. The first vehicle of each day's convoys started out from the loading area at 18.00 hours, followed at 60yd (55m) intervals by the other trucks of that company. Each convoy was sub-divided into what were described as 'serials', each a minimum of five trucks. The trucks were numbered to indicate convoy position. A one minute gap was allowed between serials, and two minutes between convoys which means that it took around 30-35 minutes for a complete convoy to clear the loading area. A Jeep generally ran at the head and also at the rear of each convoy.

Each loaded vehicle left for the outbound trip with a full tank of petrol

Above: There were frequent problems with weak bridges along the supply routes. Here, a Brockway bridge-layer completes the construction of a floating pontoon bridge to allow diversion of the route away from what may have been a narrow or impassable section. *(DD)*

Left: The supply routes were only open to military traffic but the narrow roads and the conflicting demands of both the logistics and combat traffic meant that there were frequent traffic jams. This convoy consists of Jeeps, GMCs and Dodges. The presence of an armoured half-track (bottom right) suggests that it is a combat unit which has become stalled. *(PW)*

and enough in Jerrycans to complete the return journey. Where the load permitted, full Jerrycans were also loaded for delivery to a POL dump on the outbound part of the route.

The maximum speed limit, although widely disregarded, was set at 25mph (40kph). Drivers were not permitted to overtake, nor to make any unauthorised stops.

A 10 minute break was scheduled every two hours. This was set at exactly 10 minutes before each 'even' hour to allow loads to be checked and re-adjusted, also for any maintenance or running repairs. Disabled vehicles were parked at the side of the road for recovery or repair by patrolling maintenance units. Stragglers were told to join convoys hauling similar supplies and were eventually to rejoin their own units on return to St Lô.

Operations continued through the night and the absence of enemy air activity

meant that the crews were permitted to use full headlights, initially as far as Alençon and subsequently throughout the Communications Zone. Overnight bivouac areas were created around, and to the west, of Alençon covering both the outward and return routes. This allowed a change of crew at the halfway point for each run, so that drivers had the opportunity of running with the truck both empty and loaded in a single duty shift. POL and first-echelon maintenance facilities were also provided for the vehicles at the bivouac areas.

Traffic control points were established at each of the towns through which the trucks passed. Military Police, occasionally French civilian auxiliaries, would record the movement of the convoys and supposedly check the cargo and destination. They would also direct convoy commanders to water and refuelling points. Vehicle maintenance

Above: It was the responsibility of the US Corps of Engineers to keep the supply routes open and one battalion of a general service regiment was assigned to the task of road maintenance. The M1 heavy crawler tractor was typical of the equipment that would have been used for heavy clearance including tree removal, scraper towing and bulldozing; the blade was controlled by a winch at the rear. The M1 was built by Caterpillar, Allis-Chalmers and International. *(ST)*

Left: Production of the standardised 2$\frac{1}{2}$-ton GMC started in 1941 and continued to the end of the war. Early production vehicles were fitted with an enclosed steel cab but this was eventually replaced by a simple open-topped cab. *(JB)*

companies, including four 'heavy units', were initially stationed in eight principal towns along the route to provide repair facilities and to hold replacement vehicles. These towns included St Lô, Vire, Alençon, Mortagne, Chartres, Nogent-le-Rotrou, Mayenne and Mortain. The routes were regularly patrolled by service and recovery units operating out of these eight towns. Recovery vehicles were also positioned along the route and spotter planes were used to locate disabled vehicles.

The US Army Signal Corps provided radio communications between the bivouac areas and the dispersal points. Medical aid and evacuation facilities were available from bivouac areas; a first aid kit was placed in every vehicle involved in the operation. Ambulances were available for emergency evacuation. Communication

Left: The advancing forces required huge quantities of supplies to enable them to maintain their forward momentum. The US First Army required 5,500 tons (5,588,275 Kg) of supplies a day, including 2,200 tons (2,235,310 Kg) of POL and 1,100 tons (1,117,655 Kg) of ammunition; the US Third Army requested 6,000 tons (6,096,300 Kg), including 1,411 tons (1,433,646 Kg) of POL and 2,545 tons (2,585,847 Kg) of ammunition. Patton also wanted a further 12,500 tons (12,700 tonnes) of clothing, weapons and construction materials and a further 15,000 tons (15,240 tonnes) of ammunition for reserve stocks. *(NA)*

between regulating stations and individual supply dumps was by dispatch rider.

There was no question that any of the routes could be closed to military traffic during the operation for any reason and one battalion of a Corps of Engineers general service regiment was assigned to road maintenance, together with an attached dump-truck platoon equipped for laying road surfaces. The routes had previously been marked out with thousands of road markers in French and English warning unauthorised military and civilian traffic to keep clear, unless permission had first been obtained from ADSEC. Exceptions were made for urgent military traffic and for civil authority traffic en-route for Paris. Nevertheless, there were many instances of traffic attempting to run contra to the main flow.

For the first few days of the operation, many of the convoy drivers scarcely knew where they were going and how to get there. This was not helped by the fact that trucks were being waylaid and diverted to division supply points by the advancing armies, which often resulted in convoys becoming apparently 'lost'. The speed of advance was such that, within a week of establishing the operation, ADSEC found that trucks were having to travel greater distances to reach the army dumps. In some cases drivers were actually unable to find the location to which they were supposed to deliver because it had been moved whilst the convoy was on the road. In other cases, convoy crews strayed from the designated routes, using others that were more to their liking. It was also being reported that convoy discipline was so poor that only 30% of trucks were actually travelling in organised convoys.

Although the designated terminus was at Chartres, convoys were regularly diverted from the dumps west of the Seine to new locations, sometimes as much as 100 miles (161km) further east. This increased the average turn-around times by as much as 30%, thus extending the round trip to more than 50 hours.

By 1 September, the first phase of the operation was supposed to have been completed, but the railway system had failed to cope with the assigned volume, so the target for road deliveries had been increased accordingly. The trucks continued to roll, day and night for another four days. It was not until 5 September that the first phase of the operation was considered to have been completed. By this time, almost 89,000 tons (90,424 tonnes) of supplies had been transported by road from

Above: The heavy automotive maintenance companies assigned to the supply routes were each issued with two Diamond T Model 969 medium recovery vehicles. The roadside sign suggests that this photograph was taken on the ABC route. *(TM)*

Left: Supplies being distributed from Cherbourg. The heavy dockyard crane in the background has survived the Allied bombardment. *(IWM/USE)*

Above: The supply
routes were planned to
run on many minor
'departmental' roads and
all civilian traffic was
banned from these roads
for the duration.
Thousands of these signs
were erected along the
route. and MPs were
empowered to turn back
all civilian vehicles.
(IWM/USE)

Normandy to railheads at Chartres and
Dreux, including:

- 15,040 tons (15,281 tonnes) of Class I
  supplies
- 27,232 tons (27,760 tonnes) of Class II
  supplies
- 19,047 tons (19,352 tonnes) of Class III
  supplies
- 2,559 tons (2,600 tonnes) of Class IV
  supplies
- 25,061 tons (25,462 tonnes) of Class V
  supplies

In addition, 48,000 tons (48,768
tonnes) of mixed supplies had been
moved from the railheads at Le Mans,
Chartres and Dreux.

These figures do not include vehicle
parts and other maintenance needs. For
these supplies, the Ordnance depots had to
rely on using cargo space in replacement
vehicles being delivered to the depot at
Fontainebleau.

At the end of the first phase, Colonel
Richmond was replaced by Colonel Ross
B. Warren.

Red Ball Express - Phase Two

The first phase of the operation may have
been successfully concluded by 5
September but necessity dictated that it
be extended further and, on 6 September,
the Red Ball Express entered a second,
lengthier phase of operation.

On 11 September, the route was
both extended and changed, continuing
eastward through Versailles where it
divided in two, to serve the advancing
First and Third Armies.

The first of the new branches, which
was dedicated to the support of the
First Army, took a more northerly route
from Vire than the original, using the
D524 and D924 to Argentan, the N26

to l'Aigle and Verneuil-sur-Avre. Then on the N12 to Dreux and Versailles, bypassing Paris via what is now the suburb of St Denis, before finally taking the N2 to Soissons. The return loop was directed along the D1 to Chateau-Thierry, then the D222, D402, N36 and N6 to Fontainebleau, before turning west on the D837 to Etampes and Alençon. Here it joined the original route through Domfront and Vire back to St Lô.

In support of the Third Army, the second branch went eastwards from Versailles on the N304 and N34 towards Melun and Rozay-en-Brie then to Sommesous. This route also returned via Fontainebleau. Within a week, the construction of a roadbridge at Chennevières, southeast of Paris, allowed a more direct route to be adopted, saving 16 miles (26km).

At the same time, additional base sections were created and given area command. By the beginning of October, the Red Ball Express passed through as many as five such sections, each with responsibility for co-ordinating changes to the routes, traffic control and road and vehicle maintenance. Traffic control points were established at distances of no more than 50 miles (80km) apart.

The new base sections did not always immediately assume responsibility for all of the functions associated with Red Ball. The administrative burden also began to look as though it might overwhelm the operation. ADSEC attempted to exercise overall control of movement along the entire Red Ball route, but was frequently criticised by other commanders for its actions.

By the first week of September, 115 of a total of 130 truck companies which were

assigned to the AS MTB, were involved in the Red Ball Express. A further 55 truck companies were also assigned to COMZ elsewhere, clearing ports and delivering supplies forward of the railheads. ADSEC had achieved this total by taking – often drastic – actions elsewhere. For example, activities at the beachheads were reduced by 50% and ADSEC prohibited the shipping of further supplies from Great Britain unless it could be shown that there was an urgent operational requirement. Additional provisional truck companies were created from both combat and service units. In the Normandy Base Section, two engineer general service regiments were converted into 14 truck companies, and a chemical smoke-generating battalion was issued with GMCs and reorganised as a truck battalion. Ten more companies were created from anti-aircraft units, for which there was little demand, and three infantry divisions (26th, 95th and 104th) were demobilised. The vehicles being used to form more than 40 provisional truck companies.

On 15 September, COMZ assigned the operation to ADSEC, placing it under the control of the Commanding Officer,

Motor Transport Brigade. Routes and tonnages were allocated by COMZ-G4.

On 19-20 September ADSEC informed COMZ-G4 that the northern route would be extended from Soissons to Hirson, still in support of the First Army. The return route via Soissons and Chateau Thierry was discontinued. By the time these changes took place on 1 October, the round trip distance stood at 686 miles (1,104km) on the northern route, with the figure for the southern route standing at 590 miles (949.5km). A round trip was now taking approximately 72 hours to complete... with the trucks running non-stop!

As the advancing armies passed Paris, the generally better condition of the railway northeast of the city, combined with ample rolling stock, made it easier to shift supplies by rail. This could potentially reduce the need for Red Ball operations. The US Third Army opened the first railhead on 15 September at Verdun. By the end of that month the strain on the Red Ball routes was lifted by the establishment of other rail transfer points in the Paris area. One transfer point was set up at Aubervilliers-la-Courneuve to supply the US First Army. The second transfer point was at Vincennes-Fontenay for the

Above: A combination of fatigue, driving at night under black-out conditions and the desire to press on and get the job done meant that accidents were a frequent occurrence along the route. Here, a Diamond T Model 969 medium wrecker is being used to right a GMC CCKW. The vehicle's load of Jerrycans has been spread across the road and is blocking an approaching convoy. *(TM)*

Third Army, both in well-developed yards where the trucks could load directly onto goods wagons. A third railhead opened in early October at Ruilly to service supplies for the US Ninth Army.

It was planned to carry a minimum of 4,000 tons (4,064 tonnes) of supplies a day from Normandy to Paris by rail, with 3,000 tons (3,048 tonnes) to continue by truck to forward areas. To service the rail transfer points, a diversion depot was established on the Red Ball Highway at Trappes, approximately 20 miles (32km) south of Paris, where supplies were either

two-way traffic on the Soissons-Laon-Hirson sector, and restoring the Soissons to Chateau Thierry return route. It was even suggested that all Red Ball convoys beyond Paris could be discontinued by 20 September, although this did not actually happen until 1 November. With the abandonment of the sectors east of Paris, the return journeys to the west were made on the Paris-Ablis-Chartres road.

Whenever changes were made to the routes, a maintenance crew, equipped with recovery vehicles, followed the last convoy on both the outward-bound and return sections, picking up abandoned vehicles and removing signs.

During November, the situation had improved to the point where the armies received more POL than had been requested, and the Third Army was able to make requests for specific items instead of taking 'pot luck'.

The second phase came to an end on 16 November when the supplies emergency was deemed to be over; the Normandy beachheads were closed down on the same day. At the peak of operations, the Red Ball Express employed 5,178 trucks and some 323,500 tons (328,676 tonnes) of supplies were carried on the full-length runs from Normandy to the forward depots, or to Paris for transfer by rail. The total carried in the second phase included:

- 66,477 tons (67,541 tonnes) of Class I supplies
- 74,729 tons (75,925 tonnes) of Class II supplies
- 98,682 tons (100,261 tonnes) of Class III supplies
- 30,633 tons of (31,123 tonnes) Class IV supplies
- 52,783 tons of (53,628 tonnes) Class V supplies

Left: Accidents had a habit of escalating. In this photograph, an M1A1 heavy wrecker (Ward LaFrance or Kenworth) has left the road and ended up in a ditch. Two heavy armoured recovery vehicles constructed on the chassis of the M3 Lee/Grant medium tank are being used to recover the vehicle. *(TM)*

re-routed to the railways or continued by road to regulating stations.

During October, the Third Army alone received approximately 97,955 tons (99,522 tonnes) of supplies, much arriving by rail.

The northern Red Ball route was changed again on 15 October, allowing

Right: The PLUTO project brought fuel across from the Isle of Wight, in southern England, using pipes laid on the sea bed. The fuel was then pumped to the US fuel farm at Mont Cauvin through pipeleines laid along the sides of the roads. *(IWM/USE)*

The daily average was 4,552 tons to 4,908 tons (4,625 to 4,987 tonnes) for both phases of the operation - and the best performance was achieved on 18 September when 8,882 tons (9,024 tonnes) were moved. By contrast, on the last day of the operation just five truck companies were involved and the total hauled stood at just 299 tons (303,799kg).

The total of supplies moved during the 84-day life of the operation stood at 412,243 tons (418,939 tonnes); the ton-mileage for the two phases of the operation amounted to 122 million.

Petrol

It is worth emphasising the enormous amounts of fuel that were being consumed by the advancing armies. Following the breakout from the Cotentin Peninsular on 27 July 1944, the daily fuel requirement for the US First and Third Armies had been raised from 300,000 gallons (1,140,000 litres) to 600,000 gallons (2,280,000 litres). Even this was insufficient, and by late August, the two armies were consuming approximately 1,500,000 gallons (5,700,000 litres) a day and the daily requirement for the Red Ball trucks was estimated at 300,000 gallons (1,140,000 litres).

Perversely, there was no shortage of fuel in France.

During the assault stage of Operation Overlord, all vehicles landing on the assault beaches had full tanks and carried additional fuel in Jerrycans (known as 'packaged' fuel); the surplus packaged fuel was later stacked in widely-dispersed dumps. From D+15, both motor fuel and aviation spirit were being pumped ashore at Port-en-Bessin from tankers berthed outside the small harbour. Steel pipelines, of 6in (15cm) diameter were laid alongside the D6 road, carrying the fuel from

Right: The speed of the advance made it impossible for the distribution pipes, which were 6in (15 cm) in diameter, to be be laid at sufficient speed. Around 30 miles (48km) of pipe could be laid in a day but it took 10 hours for this length to be filled with fuel. Engineers were frequently called upon to deal with breaks in the pipework. These men are British sappers fitting a new valve to allow a branch to be constructed. *(IWM/USE)*

Port-en-Bessin to the US fuel 'farm' at Mont Cauvin. Additional pipelines also brought fuel from Sainte Honorine des Pertes.

By D+21 there were 7,500,000 tons (7,620,000 tonnes) of fuel and other petroleum products stockpiled in Normandy.

In late June 1944, the pipeline under the ocean (PLUTO) project had laid four reinforced 3in (76cm) diameter flexible pipes on the seabed from Sandown and Shanklin on the Isle of Wight to Cherbourg, a distance of 70 miles (113km), in just 10 hours. In January 1945, admittedly after the termination of the original Red Ball operation, these pipes were supplemented by 11 flexible pipelines and six rigid steel pipelines which were laid between Dungeness and Ambleteuse, close to Boulogne. By this time, the capacity of the pipeline system was more than 1,000,000 gallons (3,800,000 litres) a day. By the end of the war in Europe, the PLUTO project, parts of which can still be seen at Shanklin, Ambleteuse and Port-en-Bessin, had delivered 172,000,000 gallons (653,600,000 litres) of fuel.

But, the real problem lay in getting the fuel to the advancing armies. It had originally been planned that 4in (10cm) and 6in (15cm) diameter steel pipelines would continue to be laid alongside roads to fuel depots sited at strategic points. With considerable effort, it was possible for 30 miles (48km) of 6in (15cm) pipe to be laid in a day. It then required approximately 10 hours for the pipes to be filled during which time no fuel could be delivered. However, the speed of advance was often far swifter than this and the engineers could not keep up; on one notable day, the armies advanced 40 miles (64km). Also there were times when the pipelines had advanced beyond distribution points, but no fuel could

be spared to fill the pipes. Breaks in the pipeline caused interruptions to the supply and the constant need for filling newly-laid sections reduced the amount of fuel available at delivery points. On 13 September, for example, it was estimated that the pipelines contained the equivalent of 200,000 barrels of fuel.

Furthermore, large numbers of trucks were required to haul pipeline sections, which meant that these vehicles were not available for transporting other supplies.

With the armies advancing at such speed the only practical way to deliver the fuel, until the advance slowed and engineer units could catch up, was by road from the fuel 'farms', either in Jerrycans, often filled by German prisoners of war or in bulk tankers or by tanker semi-trailers.

There were also dedicated 'POL hauls' which had started on D+8 (14 June 1944) and continued throughout the European campaign. Nevertheless, the delivery of fuel remained one of the main priorities of the Red Ball Express.

Operational problems

Although it was unprecedented in the history of warfare, there is no doubt that the establishment of the Red Ball Express was a hurried affair that was plagued by control and operational problems. It achieved the objective… but only just.

In reviewing the operation, ADSEC identified deficiencies in road maintenance, handling of supplies, traffic control, communications along the extended routes and vehicle maintenance. Driving was often reckless in the extreme, with accidents a common occurrence, as much through tiredness as any other factor. British units joked that if a US convoy was seen to be approaching, it was wise to both get off the road and climb a tree!

As regards to vehicles, ADSEC concluded that 10-ton tractor and semi-trailer outfits would have been more efficient than the $2^1/_2$-ton trucks which made up the main part of the fleet. ADSEC also believed that the convoys should have been smaller than company size, with a figure of 13 to 16 vehicles being suggested as the most satisfactory for loading and dispatch.

Regular stops should also have been scheduled for meals.

But the Red Ball operation had been put into effect with minimal training and it is hardly surprising that there were problems, the most serious of which was the continual delays in loading and unloading the supplies, which extended convoy turn-around times. Although some cranes were available, there was almost no other mechanical-handling equipment. Most of the loading and unloading operations were performed by man-handling the supplies on and off the trucks.

In mid-September, an analysis of loading operations on 16 convoys at Normandy Base Section showed a variation in time of between 11^{1}/$_{2}$ and 39 hours. Things were no better at the delivery point of the route where the unloading time varied between 11 and 36 hours. There had been considerable improvement by mid-October when an analysis of 228 convoys showed that the loading figure varied between 3.7 and 18.8 hours, but the actual figure depended very much on the type of supplies being handled.

Much of the delay was caused by the dispersal of dumps at both the loading and unloading points. At the base section, supplies were frequently not placed or identified to facilitate speedy handling. Many shipments were so poorly documented that it was impossible to tell what the load was or where it was intended to be delivered. Consequently, armies often received supplies which had neither been requested nor required.

Despite the provision of hard-standings, the glutinous Normandy mud was also a problem. Vehicles became bogged down at the loading points which made it difficult to move from one loading area to another, with cranes and bulldozers being used to keep vehicles moving. German prisoners of war were frequently employed on road maintenance tasks.

There were also problems with hauling supplies which had a high bulk-to-weight ratio which could result in too few trucks being available to carry a particular load. The problem was obviated by supplying both tonnage and cubage figures for Class II and Class IV supplies; this helped the transport company requisitioning personnel to allot an appropriate number of vehicles.

Weighbridges were not available during loading operations. Similarly, there were problems associated with handling

particularly dense supplies and, despite 'Washington' having approved a 100% overloading of the trucks, the 5-ton (5,080kg) loading figure was widely ignored. A single 105mm or 155mm artillery shell weighed 100 lb (45kg), and a single layer of these stacked in crates in a long-bed GMC AFKWX would put the truck over the weight limit. Therefore it is hardly surprising that weight

restrictions were ignored and trucks were sent on the road dangerously overloaded often causing problems with brakes, transmission and tyres.

The average daily vehicle load was approximately 5.6 to 7.3 tons (5,080 to 7,417kg) which, bearing in mind that most of the vehicles in use were of the standard 2¹/₂-ton type, allows a good impression of the degree of overloading.

In the latter days of the operation, more semi-trailers were available and the problem of overloading was reduced.

Delayed vehicles were also proving to be something of a problem. An increasing number of accidents occurred as drivers attempted to catch up with the convoys.

Jerrycans also became a particular concern because drivers tended not to replace emptied cans on the truck but

Above: The driver of the Jeep lead vehicle checks the route before escorting his convoy of GMC trucks onto the road. *(PW)*

simply to throw them in the hedgerow. The road verges on the Red Ball routes eventually became littered with thousands of discarded cans, which led to a serious shortage. When linked with a similar level of carelessness on the part of the advancing armies, it should be no surprise that there was eventually such a shortage of available Jerrycans that a reward was offered to civilians for every can returned.

Standing Operating Procedure

Partly in response to the problems which were becoming evident in the control of the convoys and the general abuse of the trucks, the headquarters of the Motor Transport Brigade published on 1 October a new Standing Operating Procedure.

Each convoy was to be made up of not less than one 16-vehicle truck platoon and each truck was to be marked with a red disc of at least 6in (15cm) diameter - for example, a standard 'bridge' disc - on which the position of the vehicle in the convoy was marked by means of a number. Drivers were issued with a written notification of convoy number, route and destination.

The lead vehicle in the convoy was indicated by carrying a blue flag, and the last vehicle carried a green flag. If flags were not available, a white board with black lettering was to be used for identification. The convoy commander's vehicle was to be identified by a similar board indicating status.

The convoy was to be commanded by a commissioned officer riding in a Jeep at the rear, rather than at the head which had previously been the custom. At least one motor mechanic was to be carried in his vehicle. The commander was responsible for the safety of the cargo and to also alert personnel attempting to sell, steal or barter supplies – a common problem.

To reinforce the importance of security, drivers were made financially responsible for any loss of cargo.

At the head of the convoy was the leader, who could either be a commissioned officer or a 'reliable' non-commissioned officer (NCO). Non-commissioned officers were also to be spaced throughout the convoy in order to assert authority.

Once a convoy had been assigned to a destination, it could only be diverted by written order from a properly authorised and identified commissioned officer. The convoy commander was required to be present during the loading and unloading and was to ensure that the time spent during these parts of the operation was kept to a minimum.

On leaving the first traffic control post (TCP), all of the trucks were required to have full fuel tanks and to be carrying a minimum of 20 Jerrycans filled with petrol. Each crew member was to carry a full canteen of water and sufficient 'C rations' for the round trip.

If a vehicle should break down, the convoy commander was responsible for deciding whether or not it could be repaired by the convoy mechanic. If on-the-spot repair was determined not to be possible, then the vehicle and crew were to be left by the side of the road, to await an Ordnance maintenance patrol. Once the truck was repaired, the driver was to be given a map of the route, together with written instructions. The driver was to proceed to the next control post to be given further instructions.

Vehicles were to be spaced 60 yards (55m) apart on the open road, closing up to 15 yards (14m) apart when passing through towns or villages. The lead vehicle was not to exceed a speed of 25mph (40kph) and the closing speed of following vehicles was restricted to a maximum of 30mph (50kph). These speeds were to be reduced to

15mph (24kph) and 20mph (32kph) respectively when passing through built-up areas and the lower speeds were to be maintained until the rear vehicle in the convoy had cleared the urban area.

As before, a 10-minute halt was to be made before 'even' hours for rest and first echelon maintenance also for any adjustment to the load that might be necessary. Four 30-minute halts a day were to be made for meals: at 06.00, 12.00, 18.00 and 24.00 hours. All halts were to be made outside urban areas, with the convoy simply pulling up alongside the road. NCOs were positioned to protect the front and rear of the convoy and to direct passing traffic. No other halts were permitted unless directed by a control post, terminal or military policeman.

The convoy was to stay in column and was not allowed to pass other moving convoys.

When forward of the army rear boundaries, standard lighting procedure was to be followed, including the proper use of blackout and dipped headlights.

Above: Not all supplies were moved exclusively by road. During the first phase of the Red Ball operation, some 20,000 tons (20,320 tonnes) were intended to be delivered by rail. Five transport companies were assigned to railhead work. *(QM)*

Maintenance problems

When the Red Ball operation commenced it was believed that there was a possibility that the war would be over within weeks. It was considered that the strain, which the operation would place on the men and equipment, was a price worth paying.

There was a definite, though unwritten, decision taken to minimise maintenance of the vehicles. High Command's thinking was that driving the trucks to destruction was unimportant if the operation hastened the end of the war. Although officially sanctioned at 100%, overloading went way beyond this figure and took its toll on axles, transmissions and tyres leading to a shortage of parts. Around 100 otherwise repairable trucks had to be withdrawn from the Red Ball operation every day as a result of a shortage of parts.

By 28 September, the Ordnance Maintenance Companies (OMC) were carrying out 1,500 repairs a day, with 600 vehicles under repair having to be replaced. Around 200 of these vehicles were replaced as a result of accidents and 70 of the 200 were wrecked beyond repair. It required 72 hours to rebuild a complete vehicle from the engine; a new engine could be installed, providing one was available, in four or five hours and a clutch in 45 minutes. A transmission exchange required two hours.

But many of the problems were being caused by the lack of first and second level maintenance. Returning crews were supposed to carry out running maintenance tasks at the bivouac areas. Crews were too tired to do so and also reluctant to crawl under a truck parked in what had often become a 'sea' of mud.

Typical problems included batteries which had run dry due to a lack of distilled water. Engines and axles seized because they had not been greased or oil levels checked or topped-up. Dirt or water frequently contaminated fuel lines due to carelessness during refuelling or sabotage by the German prisoners of war employed to fill the Jerrycans. Nuts and bolts became loose, which often resulted in drive-shafts uncoupling, wheels detaching and transfer cases becoming loose. Cab and body parts often cracked as a result of vibration. Often a lack of spare parts forced mechanics to cannibalise non-operational trucks to keep others running. This further exacerbated the shortage of vehicles.

From late September, it was proposed that a service-station system be established using a pool of mechanics from the truck units to ensure that first and second level maintenance was correctly performed.

Maintenance had initially been carried out on the '40+8' system, meaning that for every 40 trucks operating, eight would be undergoing servicing by unit mechanics. Whilst this was adequate under normal operating conditions, it proved to be insufficient when trucks were being operated under such arduous conditions. Consequently it was suggested that every truck should pass through a maintenance procedure on completion of a round trip. Based on a three-day trip turnaround and a total of 7,000 vehicles at work on the route, this would have meant that 2,300 vehicles would require servicing every day. Despite being approved for implementation 'without delay' on 7 October, the plan would have been costly in both manpower and other resources and was never implemented.

Whilst the advancing armies considered the Red Ball Express to be a lifeline, to the hard-pressed maintenance men of the Ordnance Maintenance Companies, it was an extravagant use of vehicles, tyres, engines, transmissions and other parts at a time when these items were in short supply.

Tyres

Tyres came in for a particular pounding due to factors such as under-inflation, over-loading, excessive speed, rough road surfaces and general bad driving. Some 65% of tyre replacements were thought to be a direct result of driving over discarded combat ration cans on the road. The problem was eventually, at least partially, solved by sweeping the roads with a magnetic device attached to the front of a truck.

Since few of the trucks carried a spare wheel, a puncture meant that either the truck was out of action until a road patrol came by or, more commonly, it was simply driven to the nearest maintenance point on a flat tyre thereby ensuring that the tyre was ruined. Alternatively, most of the vehicles being used had twin rear wheels which meant that the wheel with the flat tyre was simply taken off the truck, adding to the overload on the remaining wheel.

It was also estimated that as many as 10% of tyres were used until they were too far worn for retreading.

In September, the OMC's tyre status report showed that consumption of 7.50x20 8-ply tyres - the size used on both the $1^1/_2$-ton Chevrolet tractor and the $2^1/_2$-ton GMC truck - was running at 55,059 against a monthly average of 29,142 in the preceding three months. This figure represented more tyres than were held in stock for the month and some 40,000 tyres of that size were awaiting repair.

By 9 October, the Transportation Corps estimated a requirement for 180,236 tyres of all sizes, over the following 75 days and that the total number of tyres available in Europe was less than 2,000, with just 46,956 available in Great Britain. Until January 1945, Ordnance had just one

Above: The trucks were driven day and night, and although the crews were supposed to undertake first ecehelon maintenance before bedding down, fatigue and other factors meant that it was rarely completed adequately. This lack of maintenance eventually became a problem and many trucks had to be taken out of service. This truck has been fitted with brackets to carry a rigid towbar which would allow the recovery of a stranded vehicle. *(QM)*

operational tyre repair company, the 158th. The 158th was split into six teams: two were attached to the First Army, two to the Third Army, and two remained with ADSEC. Tyre repair materials were sourced locally whenever possible. To help overcome what could have been a serious problem The Michelin Company in France and Engelbrecht in Belgium were awarded contracts for tyre repair; Michelin was soon repairing up to 200 tyres a day.

Nevertheless, it is not surprising that tyres became an extremely scarce commodity.

Problems with road patrols

Changes to the route also created problems, with OMC facilities not always being informed of what was occurring. This sometimes meant that unserviceable vehicles remained at the roadside for many days. For example, changes to the route were made on 11 September, but road patrols were not operational on the changed route until 19 September. This resulted in 81 loaded, but unserviceable, trucks abandoned along the road between Vire and Dreux. On 15 September, Colonel Ross B. Warren, commanding the MTB, complained to ADSEC that since 10 September there had been no road patrols conducted between Mortagne, Chartres and the River Seine. Also, that 27 companies of the 27th QM Group (TC) had no maintenance between 10 and 12 September; and that no patrols were located at the St Cyr diversion point on 10 and 11 September.

The heavy automotive maintenance companies assigned to the Red Ball route were each issued with two Diamond T Model 969 medium recovery vehicles, and two standardised M1A1 heavy recovery vehicles, either the Ward La France Model

1000 or the similar Kenworth 573. The medium automotive maintenance units were each equipped with two Diamond Ts. This proved to be insufficient and was supplemented, from 18 October, by the use of 50 Diamond T Model 980/981 tractor/trailer combinations. Contemporary sources suggest that these were semi-trailers which would indicate that the British-built Shelvoke & Drury 30-ton trailer was used with a fifth-wheel conversion on the tractor unit. This appears very unlikely and a more obvious explanation is that the word 'semi' in the

relevant document ('History of G-4 Com Z European Theater of Operations; Section III, Supply by Road, Air and Water', dated 1946) is an error and that the standard US-built 45-ton draw-bar trailers were used.

Route maintenance

The high levels of traffic also began to have a marked effect on the condition of the roads, some of which needed constant reconstruction. By late September, a reconnaissance of the route showed that the areas around Normandy Base Section and

stretches of the roads between Vire and Paris were often impassable during wet weather. There were also problems with damage to weak bridges and narrow roads in towns where it was sometimes impossible for trailers to turn often ending in an accident.

Road maintenance was the responsibility of the US Corps of Engineers headquartered at Alençon, with platoons bivouacked along the route. The task was a difficult one because the roads were in constant use and standing instructions stated that no part of the road was to be closed to traffic.

Above: Engineers battled constantly to keep the supply routes open. Here, a White or Autocar tractor towing a 10-ton (gross) van semi-trailer is waved through road repairs being carried out by the 2nd Battalion 355th US Engineers at St. Denis, France, 7 September 1944. *(NA)*

3 | They Drive by Night...

At its height, the Red Ball Express employed more than 50,000 men from the Service of Supply (SOS) and Quartermaster 'light' or 'heavy' truck companies. Around 80% of these men were African-Americans, but prisoners of war were also used to help with loading and unloading operations. Instructed to keep the convoys rolling at all costs, the toll was heavy on both men and machinery.

Right: A mixed convoy of well-loaded forward-control (AFKWX) and normal-control (CCKW) 2^1/$_2$-ton GMCs line up with 1-ton trailers at a railhead. The relaxed attitude of the crews suggests that they have yet to receive their orders. *(NA)*

Whilst it was not an exclusively 'white' army, the US Army of 1944 was, by design, strictly segregated along racial lines. A War Department policy document of 1940 had stated explicitly that 'negro units were to be provided in all arms and services of the Army', but the truth was that African-American soldiers – at the time invariably referred to as 'coloured' or 'negro' soldiers – were not allowed to serve alongside whites, and were formed into separate units. A far greater proportion of non-white draft inductees were rejected as being unfit for military service than was the case with white men and, with few exceptions, the African-Americans were also considered to be mentally and physically unfit for combat roles. Despite often protesting that they were both ready and willing to serve their country in combat, many of those men that were drafted, found themselves in relatively safe non-combat roles.

African-American soldiers were frequently assigned to supply depots where they loaded and unloaded food, ammunition and other supplies to transportation companies, ordnance units and mess halls.

The African-Americans made up only 10.3% of the strength of the US Army but, because they were generally discouraged from entering combat units, they represented 20.7% of the service units. Of 210,209 Negro soldiers serving in Europe, 93,292 were in the Ordnance Corps and approximately 73% of the Transport Companies used in the Motor Transport Service of the European Theatre were Negros; this means that most of the companies involved in the Red Ball Express were of the same ethnic origin. Of course, there were also plenty of white men on the Red Ball Express, but it seems that they did not serve together. Off-duty, they were discouraged from fraternising for fear this would lead to problems.

Thus, the white and non-white troops remained fully segregated, often with separate headquarters and command structures – although all of the troops

Above: A large percentage of the troops employed on the supply operations were African-Americans. Here, troops are loading boxed supplies which have been delivered by rail. *(IWM/USE)*

were generally commanded by white officers, any suggestions that white NCOs (non-commissioned officers) be assigned to African-American units led to the criticism that morale would be destroyed since non-white troops would see no opportunities for advancement.

At one time, it was said that more than 50,000 men were employed on the Red Ball Express, some 40,000 of them African-Americans. All of these men were initially drawn from the Service of Supply (SOS) and Quartermaster 'light' or 'heavy' truck companies. When it was found that there were insufficient drivers available, infantrymen were also encouraged to volunteer for these duties. However, many were disappointed when they were turned

down for what was regarded as a safe and 'cushy' job.

Each 'light' truck company had an establishment of five officers and 105 enlisted men, generally operating GMC $2^1/_2$-ton 6x6 cargo trucks or tankers, or, more rarely, Studebaker $2^1/_2$-ton or Chevrolet $1^1/_2$-ton tractors with semi-trailers. A 'heavy' transport company was staffed by five officers and 112 men, and was equipped with 4 to 5 ton tractor units, operated with 10-ton semi-trailers or tanker semi-trailers.

Although sometimes housed in unused schools and other public buildings, the men generally lived in tents.

Prisoners of war were also used for loading and unloading operations in rear

areas; one Gas Supply Company, based at Reims, had as many as 250 German prisoners of war cleaning windscreens, and checking tyre pressures and oil levels.

Little driver training was given, even to men who had no previous experience of driving a truck, much less one with a crash gearbox which required double de-clutching skills. Instructors considered that a man could be taught to drive in two or three days. Training methodology was to simply sit the man in the driving seat, show him which control did what and then let him get on with it. During their three days 'training', the men would also be shown how to change a wheel, how to deal with ignition and carburetion problems and how to check the various fluid levels.

The men were taught how to drive in convoy, maintaining the correct distance from the truck in front. Also, how to drive on black-out lights; although trucks could be driven on full headlights to the west of Paris – black-out lights had to be used for the last 10 miles (16km) or so, as the convoys approached the battlefront.

Additional problems arose when companies which had previously operated standard 6x6 trucks were converted to tractor-trailer outfits. This was often achieved with little more instruction than simply being allowed to practise in a field.

On an average day, 899 trucks were sent forward and continued operating 24 hours a day. The work was arduous and continuous, and generally thankless.

Above: Dense stores such as ammunition almost guaranteed that the trucks were overloaded; and although this was tolerated to a maximum 100%, providing the trucks were operating on surfaced roads, the weight often went well beyond this figure. *(TM)*

Above: African-Americans were also employed on maintenance work. *(UB)*

During the operation crews faced bad roads, the occasional air attack and extreme fatigue in their efforts to get the vital supplies to the fighting men.

The average journey time was 54 hours and many trucks operated with a single driver, snatching a sleep whenever the convoy halted. The men generally ate cold 'C' rations on the move... until it was discovered that a hot meal could be prepared by placing tinned rations on the truck's exhaust manifold! Scheduled breaks were minimal – just 10 minutes every two hours, during which the drivers were supposed to carry out light maintenance tasks on the truck.

By the time the length of a run had extended to more than 72 hours, drivers averaging 36 hours, or more, lack of sleep had became a major problem and often resulted in accidents when a driver dozed off at the wheel. Although it was not always the case, many trucks carried two drivers and, when one became too exhausted to continue, it was common practice for the two to switch places whilst the truck was on the move. At routine stops or in heavy traffic, men would doze at the wheel and drivers would gently bump the truck in front or behind to alert the sleeping driver that the convoy was ready to roll again. Often, men were driven

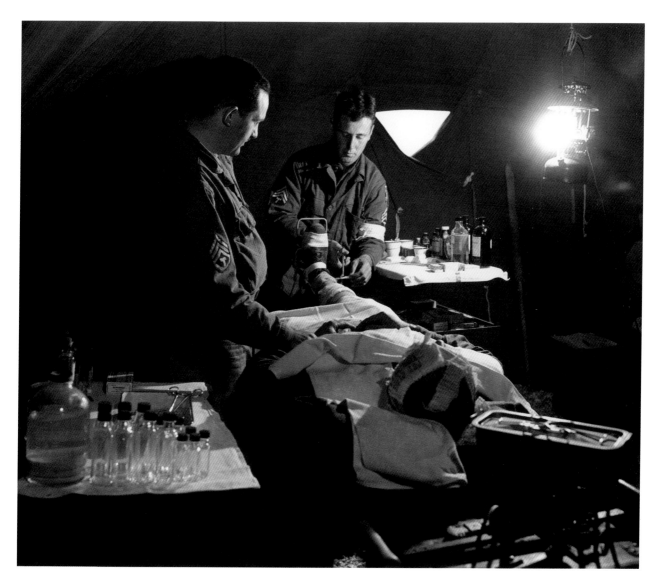

to sabotaging their vehicle in an effort to get much-needed sleep.

Speed and reckless driving were as great a cause of accidents as fatigue. There was a speed limit of 25mph (40kph) on the road, but it was widely ignored. A standard GMC 6x6 was perfectly capable of 52mph (84kph), even when loaded. Many men removed the governor from the distributor in an attempt to get more speed and it was claimed that an empty truck could reach 70mph (113kph) in this condition.

In early September 1944, in an attempt to boost morale on what was essentially an arduous and unglamorous operation,

the *Stars and Stripes* and *Yanks* newspapers carried stories about the Red Ball Express and the men who were operating the trucks. The stories were typically gushing in their praise, emphasising the difficulties of the job and telling of exhausted soldiers who 'splashed water on their faces' to enable them to continue driving, and who, 'for months on end went without mail'. There was also talk of men who 'died with their hands on the wheel', or slept on their duffel bags 'on ruins that were scarcely cooled from the heat of battle'.

Whilst perhaps a driver was more likely to be injured in a road traffic accident that

Above: A first aid kit was carried in every Red Ball Express vehicle. Ambulances were available along the route for emergency evacuation to field hospitals where more serious cases were treated. *(IWM/USE)*

Above: The open-cabbed GMC CCKW was the workhorse of the US Army. *(TM)*

Left: Almost half of the African-Americans serving in Europe were in the US Army Ordnance Corps. Approximately three quarters of the Transport Companies used in the Motor Transport Service of the European Theatre were staffed by African-Americans. As a result, most of the companies involved in the Red Ball Express were African-Americans. *(PW)*

Far left: The 10-ton (gross) refrigerated semi-trailer were equipped to maintain a temperature of between 10°F and 32°F (-5°c to 0°c) and used for transporting meat and foodstuffs. *(DD)*

was the result of someone falling asleep at the wheel, nevertheless, the men did come under fire from time to time and all Red Ball personnel carried rifles. In theory the convoys remained firmly in the communications zone but, in the early days of the operation, Red Ball drivers sometimes found themselves diverted almost to the front line. The trucks occasionally came under attack from snipers or from the air, and more than one driver recalled being forced to take cover under a hail of machine gun fire. A percentage of the trucks in each convoy were equipped with .50 calibre machine guns and, where the threat of attack was felt to be particularly serious, Dodge gun motor carriages were also positioned in the convoys, or trucks were equipped with anti-aircraft guns.

Many crews sandbagged the floor of the cab to provide some small measure of protection against mines. The threat of

mines along the verges of the route prompted drivers to drive their vehicles in the middle of the road, particularly in areas recently liberated of Germans.

Hijacking was also a potential problem, with stragglers proving particularly vulnerable.

A jerrycan of fuel could fetch $100 on the Black Market and that is where many ended up, but there were also hijackers who were closer to home than was, perhaps,

comfortable. Many of the men found the temptations too great, with petrol, cigarettes, food and sometimes whole trucks being sold to French civilians. It is probable that the Army's record-keeping was sufficiently haphazard that no one knew for sure how many trucks were operational, or indeed what they were carrying. Drivers would sometimes report to the Military Police that their truck had been stolen when, in fact, both the truck and its load

Above: Although not a common sight in Red Ball photographs, the Federal 94X43A tractor was used a towing vehicle for the 10-ton (gross) refrigerated semi-trailer. *(TM)*

On 16 September 1944, the Commander of COMZ issued this notice to the men of the Red Ball Express.

TRUCK DRIVER, RED BALL ROUTE

You and your truck are part of a team that is winning the war. It is your job to transport critical military supplies on the RED BALL ROUTE to our forces now engaged in the final destruction of the German Army. What you have done so far in supporting the attack has helped stagger the enemy.

Our armies have the Germans on the run. To keep them on the run, the supplies you carry must reach the front line at the earliest possible moment. A minute lost may give the Germans time to recover – and delay our Victory by many months.

KEEP ROLLING by obeying these rules:

1   Do not stop – unless absolutely necessary.
2   Do not pick up civilians.
3   Do not leave your truck except during rest periods.
4   Keep in line, and to your right.
5   Watch water temperature and oil pressure.
6   Inspect both truck and cargo regularly.
7   Maintain proper interval at all times – do not lag.
8   Drive steadily and carefully.

Without supplies we cannot win the war. Generals Bradley, Patton and Hodges are counting on you. Do not fail them! Get your supplies through promptly and safely. This is your part in winning a speedy Victory!

JOHN C. H. LEE
Lieutenant-General, US Army. Commanding General, COMZ

---

had been sold on the Black Market. Parked trucks always needed to be guarded and in Paris alone, some 2,000 trucks were reported as having been stolen. Drivers resorted to removing the rotor arms from the distributor when leaving trucks parked and unattended.

Fuel or ammunition-starved combat units were also known to 'divert' supplies which were meant to go elsewhere, although there was also a degree of legitimate 'trade'. One famous tale concerns the Third and Seventh Armies who found themselves just 160 miles (258km) apart. Although strictly against orders, officers of the US Seventh Army, who were short of food, proposed that they do a deal with the Third Army, exchanging two truck loads of Nazi souvenirs – helmets, pistols, dress daggers and other items that had been abandoned by the retreating Germans for two truck loads of food. The exchange took place at a Red Ball depot and for their trip across 'noman's land', the Seventh Army got two trucks full of pork, beef, cigars, 10-in-1 rations and cigarettes... and a good story into the bargain.

Returning trucks were not always empty and were sometimes required to carry Jerrycans, so many of which had been abandoned along the route that they became a scarce resource, as well as artillery

shell casings, prisoners of war and, occasionally, the bodies of the dead. The latter task was particularly unpopular because it meant that the truck beds had to be hosed clean before being used for another load; another unwelcome, and in this case distasteful, task for the hard-pressed crews.

In truth, the operation allowed little opportunity for rest or recreation. The most that many of the men could hope for was a US Clubmobile – a converted GMC truck, staffed by women volunteers of the American Red Cross, which served hot coffee and doughnuts. There were also travelling USO and 'Jeep Shows', the latter

manned by two soldier-performers carrying their kit in a Jeep trailer, who entertained the off-duty men.

Despite all towns being strictly off-limits, and with no recreational passes issued, men who were not operational would find ways of sneaking trucks out of the bivouac areas for an illegal night in a local town, some even finding time for a night or two in Paris looking for alcohol and female company. Prostitutes were a problem and many men were forced to report sick with venereal disease.

All these problems aside, the Red Ball Express managed to keep the advancing armies supplied and undoubtedly

Above: The original design for the jerrycan is said to be Italian but it was adopted by the *Wehrmacht* and then copied by the British and US forces. Millions were produced and prisoners of war were frequently employed filling the cans from bulk storage. *(NA)*

contributed to a speedy end to the war in Europe. For this reason, it is astonishing that it was not until June 2004 that the US Senate and the House of Representatives passed concurrent resolutions (Resolution 439) honouring the 'gallant African-American war heroes who served in the Red Ball Express'.

The US Transportation Corps

The US Army Expeditionary Force that was deployed to France during World War One in 1917 had demonstrated the value of bringing transportation functions together under a single command. W. W. Attebury, a former railway executive was appointed as the Director General of Transportation and, in 1918, a separate Transportation Corps was established.

With the return to peace, the Corps was

stood down, its functions being undertaken by the Transportation Division of the Office of the Quartermaster General (QMG). However, the Transportation Section of the War Department Supply Division (known as G-4) also exercised General Staff supervision over Army- wide transportation functions. In the inter-war period, G-4's only officer was Major Frank S. Ross, and the only other staff member was a secretary. In March 1941, Lieutenant-Colonel Charles P. Gross was appointed chief of the section with Ross as his deputy. Ross went on to become the man responsible for all aspects of transportation, including road, rail, sea and air in the European Theatre of Operation.

When Japan attacked the Sixth Fleet at Pearl Harbor, the US began to mobilise men on an unprecedented scale. Within three months in March 1942, the transportation functions previously carried out by G-4, the

Above: A restored GMC fitted with a Number 7 set crane. *(PW)*

Left: By late September 1944, the Ordnance Maintenance Companies were carrying out 1,500 repairs a day, with 600 of the vehicles under repair having to be replaced. It took 72 hours to rebuild a complete vehicle from the engine up; a new engine could be installed in four or five hours and a clutch in 45 minutes. A transmission change required two hours. *(PW)*

Right: Tyres came in for a particular beating due to factors such as under-inflation, over-loading, excessive speed, bad road surfaces, and general bad driving. Tyre repair materials were sourced locally whenever possible and the French Michelin Company and Engelbrecht in Belgium were given contracts for tyre repair. These trucks are at a 'Service Station' near St. Denis, France, 7 September 1944. *(NA)*

Above and left: This is the only authentic GMC Clubmobile thought to exist. These vehicles were operated by American Red Cross personnel who served hot coffee and freshly-cooked doughnuts to the men, reminding them, at least, some of the comforts of home. *(ST)*

Far left: One in four GMC trucks off the production line were fitted with an anti-aircraft machine-gun mount... and a percentage of trucks in each convoy were equipped with .50in-calibre Browning heavy machine guns. *(JB)*

Above: US Army troops filling Jerrycans. They are using a pumping trailer which is drawing fuel from a bulk tanker. The towing vehicle is a White or Autocar tractor. *(MT)*

QMG and War Department transport staff were consolidated into the Transportation Division of the newly-created Services of Supply; it was quickly redesignated as the Transportation Service and then, on 31 July, President Roosevelt established the Transportation Corps. At first, the Corps had only 'temporary' status, and was assigned all of the responsibilities and resources which had previously been given to the Transportation Service.

In November 1942, the Corps also assumed responsibility for railway operations and maintenance, previously the province of the Corps of Engineers.

Between 1942 and 1945, the US Army Transportation Corps conducted operations around the world, from the North African deserts, the islands and jungles of Southeast Asia, across the beaches of Normandy and throughout Europe. By the end of the war, the Transportation Corps had moved more than 30,000,000 troops within the continental United States and 7,000,000 soldiers plus 126,000,000 tons (128,016,000 tonnes) of supplies overseas, playing a decisive part in the Allied victory. Curiously, throughout these years the Transport Companies retained the Quartermaster designation, although the letters '(TC)' were frequently appended to the company descriptions.

In 1946, the School of Transportation was opened at Fort Eustis, Virginia, where the Corps currently has its headquarters.

When the Soviet Union blockaded the city of Berlin in 1948, the Transportation Corps organised the airlift which helped to sustain the city. Two years later, on 28 June 1950, eight years after its creation, President

Truman established the Transportation Corps as a permanent branch of the US Army.

During the Korean War (25 June 1950), the Transportation Corps kept UN and US forces supplied with food, ammunition, equipment and fuel through three savage winters. By the time the armistice was signed (27 July 1953), the Corps had shifted more than 7,000,000 tons (7,112,000 tonnes) of cargo and 3,000,000 men.

As US involvement in Southeast Asia escalated during the 1960s, the Corps provided continuous support for US forces using water craft, amphibians, trucks and transport aircraft.

On 31 July 1986, the Transportation Corps was inducted into the US Army Regimental System, with regimental insignia bearing the words 'Spearhead of Logistics'. The regiment's mission statement asserts that 'Transportation Corps officers develop concepts and doctrine to perform transportation services and support functions for forces across the operational spectrum of the National Military Strategy. Transportation officers plan, schedule and supervise the use of each mode of transportation for the effective movement of personnel and cargo'.

Since 1986, the Transportation Corps has conducted successful, and sometimes on-going, operations in Iraq, Somalia, Rwanda, Haiti and Bosnia.

At the time of writing, the Transportation Corps is the third smallest branch of the US Army, but the spirit of the Red Ball Express, and sometimes its name, lives on!

Above: Truck canopies used as temporary bivouac accomodation for units on the Red Ball route. *(IWM/USE)*

4 | 'A Red Ball by Any Other Name…'

Not all of the trucking operations during the European campaign were covered by the Red Ball Express. In truth, the tonnage hauled on the Red Ball was overshadowed by the later XYZ Express which supported the final push into Germany. But there were also other operations which followed in the footsteps of the Red Ball and were to benefit from the lessons learned.

Right: US Army transport units on snow covered roads in the area of the Belgian border, December 1944. *(MT)*

The Red Ball Express was not the only high-speed trucking operation of the War. Although the tonnage hauled by the Red Ball Express was overshadowed by the so-called XYZ Express (see page 101) which was devised to support the final push into Germany in the spring of 1945, many still believe that all trucking operations during the European campaign were covered by the Red Ball Express. Even the Transportation Corps occasionally laboured under this misapprehension.

Immortalised in the services' newspapers, the *Stars and Stripes* and *Yanks*, eulogised in song in the Broadway musical, *Call Me Mister*, and brought to life on the big screen in the eponymous Hollywood film starring Jeff Chandler and a young Sydney Poitier, the Red Ball Express appeared to have caught the imagination of the US public. There have even been two novels set against a backdrop of the operation.

However, there were other operations which followed in the tracks of the Red Ball and which benefited from the lessons learned during the 82 days of the original operation.

On 2 December 1944, more than two weeks after phase two of the original Red Ball operation had come to an end, a new Standing Operating Procedure (SOP) was issued. SOP Number 53, Red Ball Motor Transport Operations, was signed by Ross B. Warren, Colonel of the Transportation Corps. The document outlined operations 'pertaining to Red Ball or similar line of communication, movement of supplies and personnel by motor transportation'. It was based on experiences that had been gained during the operation of the Red Ball Express, and attempted to clarify the responsibilities of COMZ-HQ and the COMZ sections and correct many of the weaknesses in the original convoy operation.

Some of the important changes included the following provisions:

- Convoys were not to consist of less than the standard platoon of 20 trucks.
- The convoy commander was ordered to always ride at the rear of the convoy.

Above: Many of the supply dumps were away from hardstandings and trucks frequently became bogged down in the Normandy mud. Cranes and bulldozers were commonly used to keep vehicles moving. *(TM)*

- All convoys not marked as 'Red Ball' were to be checked at traffic control posts for proper clearance.
- Red Ball vehicles found off the authorised route were to be checked and, if found not to be on official business, were to be reported to the appropriate headquarters for disciplinary action.
- Straggler vehicles, whether empty or loaded, were to be taken by the Military Police to the nearest traffic control point and held there until they were able to join a convoy going to the appropriate destination.
- Drivers of disabled vehicles which had been abandoned by the roadside and subsequently repaired were to be issued with a certificate showing the time and date of the repairs.
- Drivers of vehicles that had been turned in to Ordnance maintenance depots were to remain with the original vehicle until a properly-documented receipt was obtained for the replacement vehicle.
- If a driver was injured or was otherwise unable to stay with his vehicle for any reason, the vehicle commander was to be left in charge of the vehicle.
- Vehicles were prohibited from dropping out of a convoy without written authorisation, which was to include the reason for leaving the convoy.
- Emergency refuelling facilities were to be provided by the Motor Transport Service which was also to ensure that all convoys were issued with sufficient fuel to complete their mission.
- No civilians were to be carried on Red Ball trucks.

- Emergency vehicles were not necessarily to be bound by the one-way working rules; this included fire-fighting vehicles, ambulances, Military Police and Ordnance patrols.
- The diversion of truck companies, battalions or groups from Red Ball operation was only to be made under the authority of HQ-COMZ.

Most of these changes were made in an effort to tighten up on discipline and to prevent drivers and crews from evading their duties as well as stealing or selling trucks and supplies.

It was also pointed out that the use of 10-ton tractor-trailer outfits was considerably more efficient than standard $2^1/_2$-ton trucks, and that the closest co-ordination was required among all involved parties to provide adequate signal communications between the forward areas, intermediate control points and the beachheads.

Red Lion Express

Also known as 'BB' (Bayeux-Brussels), the Red Lion Express Route was established to haul a daily total of 500 tons (508,025kg) of British petrol and US supplies from Bayeux to the British 21st Army Group railhead in Brussels, in order to provide additional support for Operation Market Garden in the Netherlands. The US Army provided standard $2^1/_2$-ton 6x6 trucks and experienced operating personnel, averaging eight companies, seconded from the Red Ball operation. The trucks were marked 'BB' on the windscreen. The British provided camp sites at Les Taillers, Thibauville and Boisny, and control points

Above: Discarded ration cans became a hazard along the routes, the metal tending to shred tyres, and so a number of 'road sweeper' vehicles were equipped with a beam magnet to clear the surface. *(TM)*

at Crasc and elsewhere. The British were also responsible for rations, water and other supplies.

The operation was initiated on 13 September 1944, with the first trucks travelling along the route three days later; the operation had been intended to terminate on 5 October but was extended for another week, running for a total of 26 days and terminated on 12 October. By that time, 17,556 tons (17,837 tonnes) had been moved, of which 9,631 tons (9,785 tonnes) were by the British.

The Red Lion operation was considered to be a success, hauling an average daily figure of 627 tons (637,063kg) against a target of 500 tons (508,025kg); a peak load of 1,644 tons (1,670 tonnes) was carried on 20 September. The average round trip was 720 miles (1,159km).

White Ball Express

The White Ball operation commenced on 6 October 1944 and ran for 93 days, closing down on 6 January 1945. The purpose of the operation was to shorten the lines of communication to the armies and the intermediate COMZ depots by taking supplies directly from the French port of Le Havre and the city of Rouen to various rail transfer points. The route had several branches; one ran from Le Havre through Rouen to Paris, a distance of 130 miles (209km); another, from Rouen to

Left: It was impossible for the Allied advance to continue without fuel. Patton summed up the situation admirably in a conversation with Eisenhower on 2 September 1944: 'my men can eat their belts, but my tanks gotta have gas'. *(ST)*

Rheims, which was 145 miles (233km), or to Beauvais which involved a further 50 miles (80.5km). Supplies were then either carried further forward by road, or transferred to the rail network.

A bivouac area was established 25 miles (40km) from Rouen.

The average number of transport companies involved was 29, with a peak of 48, and the average daily haul was 1,473 tons (1,497 tonnes) over an average outward trip of 113 miles (182km); total tonnage was 143,067 (145,356 tonnes), giving a total of 16,166,751 ton miles.

During the first few weeks of operation there were complaints that ADSEC was sending the trucks beyond the depot at Rheims and using the vehicles for local transport; this had a bad effect on productivity.

Green Diamond Express

The Green Diamond route was intended to haul supplies from the ports and beachhead dumps in Normandy to Avranches and Dol-de-Bretagne for transfer to the rail network. The operation was activated on 10 October 1944 and ran until 1 November, during which time 15 companies hauled 15,590 tons (15,839 tonnes) of supplies over an average 100-mile (161km) forward route.

The operation was controlled entirely by the Normandy Base Section. The crews' bivouac area, and Group headquarters,

were located at Brehal, to the north of Granville.

Confusion as to who had responsibility for initiating movements, unsatisfactory command and supervision, meant the operation was not considered to be a complete success. Thick mud at the beachhead dumps also made it difficult to operate tractor-trailer units.

ABC Haul

Although it was known as the 'ABC Haul', there is some doubt as to whether this was intended to indicate American-British-Canadian or Antwerp-Brussels-Charleroi.

The operation, which started on 30 November 1944, was intended to help clear the port of Antwerp. It carried supplies to forward depots, initially at Liege, and subsequently at Charleroi and Mons, in support of the Allied armies

pursuing the *Wehrmacht* retreat into the Ardennes.

A total of 16 truck companies were involved, using 4 to 5 ton tractor units with 10 ton semi-trailers, provided in the ratio of two trailers for every tractor unit; an average 14 companies were used for road operations, whilst two were retained for port clearance.

The operation was run as a three-part shuttle system, using a fresh driver for each stage of the trip. A marshalling yard, known as a 'surge pool', was established at Antwerp to which the two port-clearance companies carried supplies from the port. The transport vehicles did not wait in the marshalling area but simply detached the full trailer and returned to the port with an empty; this minimised waiting time at the loading point. Thirteen of the road companies were used to pick up loaded trailers from the marshalling area

Above: The ABC route (American-British-Canadian) started on 30 November 1944 and ran between Antwerp, Brussels and Charleroi. It was operated exclusively by 4-5 ton International tractors with 10-ton semi-trailers. *(TM)*

Left: Both the Alllied and Axis armies used Jerrycans and they were vital in getting fuel to the fighting men. No one was too fussy about whose cans they actually used, and here, a British soldier inspects an enormous stack of cans waiting for refilling. *(IWM/USE)*

and transport them to one of the forward depots, returning with an empty trailer to a half-way point close to Tirlemont. Here the transports were formed into serials to return the empty trailers to the marshalling yard. A third shuttle operation, using one company, or more if required, transported trailers to the depots and dumps established by the advancing armies, subsequently moving empty trailers back to the forward depots. This system was found to give a good control over the flow of supplies into the dumps and depots, matching the unloading capacity and thus minimising turnaround times.

Bivouac and ordnance maintenance facilities were provided at the halfway point. Trucks were serviced on a duty-roster basis with 7% of the fleet always out of service for preventive maintenance.

The operation closed on 26 March 1945 having been working for 117 days.

By this time, 244,924 tons (248,843 tonnes) of supplies had been moved by a daily average of 241 trucks, travelling an average of 100 miles (161km) to the forward area, carrying an average 8.7 tons (8,840kg). This gave a total forward ton-mileage of 24,492,000.

Little Red Ball

The Little Red Ball commenced operation on 15 December 1944 and ran from Cherbourg to Paris on a three-day turnaround. The operation was terminated on 17 January 1945.

The target was to carry 100 tons (101,605kg) of high-priority supplies a day using 48 4 to 5 ton tractor units and 90 10-ton semi-trailers, the larger number of semi-trailers being intended to speed the turnaround.

By the end of the operation, 3,507 tons (3,563 tonnes) of supplies had been carried, giving a daily average of 106 tons.

Right: From late September 1944, it was proposed that 'Service Stations' be established using a pool of mechanics from the truck units. This emergency service station simply occupies space beside the road in a French town. *(DD)*

Above: Although originally intended as a prime mover for tank-transporter trailers, the 40-ton Diamond T Model 980/981 was employed on the Red Ball operation. The standard semi-trailer was adapted to carry ammunition and other dense stores by welding decking between the runways. *(NA)*

Right: A more common semi-trailer for the International tractor was the 10-ton (gross) cargo trailer as seen here on the ABC route in December 1944. *(QM)*

Above: On the so-called POL hauls, 5-ton International tractors were coupled to semi-trailers carrying four 750-gallon (2,850 litre) skid tanks. *(QM)*

XYZ Express

In February 1945, it appeared as though the collapse of German Army would result in a rapid advance into the northern area. COMZ-HQ ordered ADSEC to prepare a transportation plan to support such an advance, prioritising the provision of supplies to the forward areas as follows:

Priority 1: packaged POL and minimum, essential ammunition
Priority 2: hard rations
Priority 3: signal communications supplies
Priority 4: engineer bridging and road maintenance supplies

The resulting three-stage plan for the support of the armies was known as the 'XYZ plan', commencing on 25 March 1945 and terminating on 31 May.

'Plan X' initially provided sufficient truck capacity, which was stated to be 120 $2^{1}/_{2}$-ton 'equivalent' companies, to haul daily totals of 8,000 tons (8,128 tonnes) of supplies and 4,100 tons (4,166 tonnes) of bulk POL over a distance of 150 miles (241km) on a two-day turnaround. By 31 March, 'Plan X' had been superseded by 'Plan Y' and 'Plan Z', in which the totals were increased to 30,000 tons (30,480 tonnes) of supplies and 12,300 tons (12,497 tonnes) of bulk POL a day. These totals required an 'equivalent' of 515 $2^{1}/_{2}$-ton truck companies. On 12 April, supplementary plans 'TDG-1' and 'TDG-2' brought in a further fifty $2^{1}/_{2}$-ton 'equivalent' companies.

POL was moved in two stages, the bulk POL companies used tankers to move the

fuel from the pipeheads to a distribution area. Cargo trucks were then used to move packaged POL to army supply points.

Lessons learned during the original Red Ball Express ensured that discipline and control were much improved. The trucks were controlled by four Highway Transport Divisions, and operated in platoon-sized convoys from the railheads and pipeheads in rear areas, the supplies being delivered to the First, Third, Seventh and Ninth US Army forward depots. Four separate routes were operated, initially from Liege, Duren, Luxembourg and Nancy and then into Germany.

'XYZ', was probably considered the most successful of the special European trucking operations. It moved a total of 871,895 tons (885,845 tonnes) of supplies during its 68 day life (630,000 tons [640,080 tonnes]

by VE Day, 8 May 1945), generally using 10-ton tractor-trailer combinations. The daily average was 12,895 tons (13,101 tonnes) and total ton-mileage for the operation was 111,710,479.

Yellow Diamond Route

Shortly after the XYZ Express was initiated, it was realised that the distances involved meant that it would not be possible for a single highway transport division (HTD) to handle the transport for two armies. In early April 1945, a third HTD was established to service the First Army. At the same time, a quartermaster group was assigned to the Continental ADSEC to service the Seventh Army along what was known as the Yellow Diamond Route.

Left: Jeeps were frequently deployed as the lead vehicle for a convoy. These supply trucks have been held up to allow tank transporters to pass. One of the trucks is loaded with French refugees returning to their homes near Rozay, 15 September 1944. *(NA)*

Below: Open and closed cab GMC trucks. Note that the vehicle in the centre is equipped with a winch. *(QM)*

Right: Although the Allies generally enjoyed air superiority in the months following the D-Day landings, most convoys included air-defence vehicles. The GMC truck at the rear of this line of trucks is towing an M51 multiple .50in-calibre machine gun: the so-called 'Quad Fifty' - four machine guns in the M45 mount on a four-wheeled trailer. *(MT)*

Below: The supply routes continued to run regardless of weather and it is hard to imagine how cold the vehicle occupants would get in open cabs without heaters. *(MT)*

POL Hauls

The so-called POL Hauls were routine services which started on 14 June 1944 and continued throughout the European campaign. Initially organised to supply petroleum products during the critical phases of the invasion, the POL routes either ran from ports, or subsequently, from pipeheads. The cargo was usually MT-80 motor transport fuel and AV-100 aircraft fuel.

By mid-November 1944, the POL truck fleet was made of 14 truck companies, five of which were equipped with 750-gallon (2,850 litre) tankers on the GMC 2¹/₂-ton chassis and nine of which had tractor-trailer combinations, carrying 4,000 gallons (15,200 litre) using a 2,000-gallon (7,600 litre) semi-trailer together with a 2,000-gallon (7,600 litre) full trailer. In addition, GMC 2¹/₂-ton trucks were employed to carry fuel, which was either 'packaged' in Jerrycans or loaded into 750-gallon (2,850 litre) skid tanks; these vehicles were also supplemented by tractor-trailer units equipped to carry four 750-gallon (2,850 litre) skid tanks.

Between 14 June and 31 December 1944, 423,434 tons (430,209 tonnes) of petroleum products were carried by the Motor Transport Service... totalling more than 123,000,000 gallons (467,400,000 litres)!

...and after the War

Armies continue to rely on fuel, food and ammunition to fight and, not surprisingly, since the end of World War Two, there have been similar express trucking operations in Korea, Vietnam and the Gulf. The lessons learned during the Red Ball Express are as relevant today as they were by 1945.

5 | Trucks on the 'Red Ball Express'

At the height of the Red Ball Express, 598 vehicles were at work on the route each day. The 'light' truck companies operated $1^1/_2$- or $2^1/_2$-ton cargo trucks, tankers or $2^1/_2$-ton tractors which coupled to a range of 6-ton semi-trailers. The 'heavy' transport companies were equipped with 4 to 5 ton or 5-ton 'truck-tractors' coupled to 10- or 12-ton semi-trailers or tankers.

Right: Autocar U-7144T 4x4 tractor for 10-ton (gross) semi-trailers; similar vehicles were also made by White under the designation 444T. *(PW)*

In the final analysis, the Red Ball Express was nothing more than a trucking operation. It carried the essentials that enabled armies to continue to fight: food, motor vehicle fuel, ammunition, lubricants, clothing and sundry ordnance supplies. Note that the Red Ball did not carry troops – that operation, under the control of Quartermaster Troop Transport Companies, was called Red Horse.

The operation was run by a combination of 'light' and 'heavy' US Army Quartermaster Truck Companies. At the height of the operation, there were 598 vehicles operating on the route each day. A total of approximately 6,000 vehicles were available in the European Theatre of Operations.

A 'light' truck company was usually equipped with 48 standardised GMC $2^1/_2$-ton 6x6 cargo trucks, or 750-gallon (2,850 litre) tankers, which were constructed on the same chassis; sometimes the cargo vehicles tow a 1-ton Ben Hur trailer. The $2^1/_2$-ton

standardised cargo truck was considered as the basic vehicle for military transportation. Cargo in lift capacities were often described in terms of $2^1/_2$-ton 'equivalents'. The operation was not solely confined to the use of GMC trucks. A smaller number of companies used the Chevrolet $1^1/_2$-ton or Studebaker $2^1/_2$-ton tractor in conjunction with a range of 6 ton (36,578kg) (gross) weight semi-trailers.

The 'heavy' transport companies were equipped with 48 'truck-tractors', rated at either 4 to 5 ton or 5 ton, from a variety of manufacturers, coupled to either a 10 or 12 ton (10,160 or 12,193kg) (gross) semi-trailer, or a 2,000-gallon (7,600 litre) semi-trailer tanker; the number of semi-trailers often exceeded the number of tractors by a ratio of 2:1.

Vehicle types

On VE Day, the US Motor Transportion Corps had a total of 160 truck companies

Above: The ubiquitous GMC was not the only 2¹/₂-ton 6x6 truck used by the US Army. This is the Studebaker US6, most of which were supplied to the Soviet Union. The tractor variant of this chassis was used on the European supply routes. *(PW)*

under its control in Europe, equipped with the following vehicle types. Aside from the 10 ton Mack and White cargo vehicles, which were diesel powered, all of the other trucks used petrol engines.

Light truck companies

- 1¹/₂-ton 4x4 tractors, with 6 ton (6,096kg) (gross) cargo semi-trailers; Chevrolet G-4113, G-7113; six companies
- 2¹/₂-ton 6x6 cargo trucks; GMC CCKW; 64 companies
- 2¹/₂-ton 6x6 750-gallon (2,850 litre) tankers; GMC CCKW; five companies
- 2¹/₂-ton 6x6 forward-control cargo trucks; GMC ACKWX; 28 companies
- 2¹/₂-ton tractors, with 5 to 7 ton (gross) cargo semi-trailers; Studebaker US6; two companies

Heavy truck companies

- 4 to 5 ton tractors, with 10/12 ton (gross) cargo semi-trailers; Autocar U-7144T, IHC M425/M426; 127 companies
- 4 to 5 ton tractors, with 2,000-gallon (7,600 litre) semi-trailers; Autocar U-7144T, IHC M425/M426; 12 companies
- 5 ton tractors, with 12 ton (12,193kg) (gross) refrigerated semi-trailers; Federal 94X43; two companies
- 10 ton 6x4 cargo trucks; Mack NR9, White 1064; 14 companies

Any of these vehicles could, and would, have been found operating on the Red Ball Express and on the other express routes.

In addition, one, or perhaps two, heavy companies were equipped with converted

Diamond T M19 tractor-trailer outfits capable of carrying up to 45 tons (45,722kg). At the time this would have been considered to be a huge payload.

Other vehicles

Other vehicles that were directly involved in the operation, although not in carrying supplies, included Jeeps, used by the Convoy Commanders and medium and heavy-duty recovery vehicles, employed by Ordnance Maintenance Companies to patrol the route. Harley-Davidson motorcycles were used by dispatch riders and the Military Police, the latter being responsible for traffic control and convoy discipline.

Not dealt with here are vehicles such as anti-aircraft gun motor carriages which sometimes accompanied the convoys; cranes and bulldozers which were used to assist in loading the trucks and,

occasionally extricating them from the pervasive Normandy mud; and miscellaneous support trucks used by the Ordnance Maintenance Companies to carry parts and tools.

Autocar U-7144T, 4 to 5 ton tractor

The forward-control (cab-over engine, or COE) 4 to 5 ton 4x4 Autocar U-7144T tractor was designed to be used with a range of 6 ton (10 ton gross) semi-trailers, or with a 2,000-gallon (7,600 litre) fuel semi-trailer. The vehicle first appeared in 1941 and remained in production until 1945, with some 11,104 examples built. The U-7144T was a standardised design, and a near identical vehicle was produced by the White Motor Company (2,751 built) under the designation Model 444T.

Above: Autocar U-4144T tractor coupled to a 2,000 gallon (7,600 litre) fuel-servicing semi-trailer and a similar capacity full trailer. Although this type was not a regular vehicle on the Red Ball route, the type might well have been used during the POL operations. *(PW)*

Right: A fine line-up of restored GMCs as part of a Red Ball re-enactment. Note the .50in-calibre Browning heavy machine gun on the third truck in line, typical of air-defence vehicles used on the supply routes. *(PR)*

Above: Open-cab variant of the Autocar U-7144T or White 444T tractor intended for use with a range of 10 ton gross semi-trailers, or with a 2,000 gallon (7,600 litre) fuel tanker semi-trailer. Almost 14,000 were built. *(DD)*

In service, the vehicles generally replaced the earlier 2¹/₂ ton Autocar U4144-T and GMC AFKX-502-8E tractors.

Early examples were fitted with a standard commercial two-door cab, which was combined with a short bonnet, simple vertical bar-type grille and basic military-style mudguards. In 1942, the closed cab was replaced by a standard open cab design with a folding windscreen, canvas top and side-screens. A steel treadplate platform was fitted across the chassis rails ahead of the fifth wheel, protecting the top of the fuel tanks and providing access to the twin spare-wheel carriers fitted behind the cab. One vehicle in four off the production line was fitted with an anti-aircraft gun mount. On closed-cab

vehicles this was the M60 or M61 mount the M36 was used on open cabs.

Regardless of origin, the truck was powered by a 8,669cc Hercules RXC six-cylinder water-cooled petrol engine driving both axles through a five-speed gearbox, with an over-drive top gear, and two-speed transfer case. Drive to the front axle could be disengaged when not required.

The suspension was thoroughly conventional: live axles suspended on semi-elliptical multi-leaf springs. Brakes were air-pressure operated and there were four air-line connections provided for the semi-trailer brakes. A hand-control valve was mounted in the cab to allow the brakes on the semi-trailer to be operated independently. Wheels of 20in (51cm)

diameter were fitted with 9.00x20 bar-grip tyres.

Trailers

A standard US Army fifth wheel was fitted, and typical semi-trailers used with this tractor on the Red Ball Express operation included:

- 5 ton (10 ton gross) refrigerator semi-trailer
- 6 ton 2,000-gallon (7,600 litre) fuel semi-trailer
- 6 ton (10 ton gross) van semi-trailer
- 7 ton (10 ton gross) cargo semi-trailer (G-596)
- 25 foot wrecking semi-trailer, Type C-2
- 12$\frac{1}{2}$-ton 40 foot wrecking semi-trailer, Type C-2

Chevrolet G-4113, G-7113, 1$\frac{1}{2}$-ton tractor

First introduced in 1940 as the G-4100 Series and superseded in 1942 by the more militarised G-7100, the 1$\frac{1}{2}$-ton Chevrolet became the US Army's standard 4x4 vehicle in this weight class throughout the war and remained in production until 1945. It was derived from a civilian vehicle of the same rating, and incorporated all-wheel drive and the usual uncompromising military-style bonnet, mudguards and radiator. The two-man cab was shared with the GMC 2$\frac{1}{2}$-tonners; the 'Chevrolet' name was embossed onto the engine side panels in early production vehicles. In this instance, unlike the GMC, there was no open cab variant.

Above: White or Autocar tractor coupled to a 4,000 gallon (15,200 litre) refueller semi-trailer. These trailers were used by the US Army Air Force to deliver fuel from the bulk distribution points to airfields. *(DD)*

Power was provided by a 3,859 Chevrolet six-cylinder water-cooled petrol engine, driving both axles through a four-speed gearbox and two-speed transfer case. Drive to the front axle could be disengaged when not required. GM 'banjo'-type hypoid axles were mounted on semi-elliptical leaf springs; the wheels were of the standard 20in (51cm) diameter and fitted with 7.50x20 bar-grip tyres. The vehicle's brakes were hydraulic, with vacuum-servo power assistance. A Warner electric brake hand controller was fitted in the cab to allow the trailer brakes to be operated separately.

Most of the production total of 168,603 were steel-bodied cargo vehicles; other variants included panel van, airfield crash truck, bomb servicing vehicle, oil servicing vehicle, telephone maintenance vehicle, airfield lighting and many other types of body. Just 169 examples were produced of the G-4113 and G-7113 tractor variants, of which only 97 were of the original G-4113 model. Both types of tractor were used on the Red Ball Express, in conjunction with a range of 6 ton (gross) semi-trailers.

Trailers

A standard US Army fifth wheel was fitted, and typical semi-trailers used with this tractor on the Red Ball operation included:
- $3^1/_2$-ton (6 ton gross) stake-sided semi-trailer
- $3^1/_2$-ton (6 ton gross) platform semi-trailer
- $3^1/_2$-ton (6 ton gross) van semi-trailer

Diamond T Model 969, 4 ton wrecker

In 1934, the US Artillery had specified a 4-ton 6x6 truck for use as a towing vehicle for the 155mm artillery pieces, and as a general stores carrier. By 1939,

Left: US Military Police were generally equipped with the Harley-Davidson WLA, a heavy solo motorcycle fitted with a 737cc V-twin side-valve engine. The MPs were deployed to keep control of the convoys. *(DD)*

Above: Autocar or White tractor with a 10-ton (gross) cargo trailer. *(DD)*

when the design was standardised for all branches of US services, Diamond T, Autocar and White were the prime suppliers. In 1941, the White and Autocar models were superseded and for the duration of the war, the Diamond T Motor Car Company of Chicago received all major contracts for the 4-ton 6x6 'standard' chassis... which included a 'medium wrecker' intended to lift, tow disabled vehicles and equipment such as trucks, light AFVs and, occasionally, aircraft.

The vehicle was initially fitted with the Diamond T Company's 1930s two-seat 'de-luxe' cab with distinctive V-shaped windscreen; the cab had originally been introduced in 1933 with just a modest windscreen slope but this had been increased to an outrageous 30° in 1936. Sadly, by late 1942, the 'de-luxe' cab had been replaced by a plain three-man open cab with a flat, two-piece hinged windscreen, canvas top and small front-hinged doors which were fitted with canvas sidescreens.

The recovery variant, or 'wrecker', was introduced in 1941, using the short-wheelbase version (151in [3.84m]) of the standard 4-ton 6x6 chassis.

Diamond T did not produce their own power units and, as with all of the 6x6 4 ton chassis, the vehicle was powered by a 8,669cc Hercules RXC six-cylinder side-valve petrol engine. The transmission was a five-speed constant-mesh unit with an overdrive top gear, driving through a two-speed transfer case to Timken double-reduction live axles front and rear. Suspension was by conventional semi-elliptical leaf springs. The vehicle was equipped with Bendix air brakes.

The vehicle was equipped with well-designed wrecking gear, supplied by Ernest Holmes of Chattanooga, Tennessee. The gear comprised of two swivel booms, each with a 5-ton winch having 200ft (61m) of cable. The two recovery winches were mounted behind the cab, and were driven from a power take-off on the transfer case. In use, the winches could be used together to give a

total pull of 10 tons (10,160kg) or could be used separately. One used to anchor the vehicle and the other to provide a 5 ton (5,080kg) pull to the side. During lifting operations telescopic legs were used to provide support and, when using only a single boom, the leg prevented the truck from being overturned. A crew of two was required to operate the controls since these were located on each side of the body, one set to each winch.

A small steel body was fitted behind the recovery gear, with the centre part of the body cut-away to provide clearance for the booms to be swung out. Snatch blocks, anchors and scotches were carried in the

Above: Studebaker US6 6x4 road-going tractor coupled to an unusual flat-bed trailer. There was also a 6x6 variant of this vehicle. *(PW)*

Left: The Diamond T Model 980/981 ballast tractor. Originally supplied to the British Army to supplement Scammell Pioneer tank transporters. The vehicle was adopted by the US Army as 'substitute standard' until the appearance of the Pacific M26 Dragon Wagon. *(PW)*

two large tool boxes forming part of the truck bed above the rear wheels. Other equipment included oxy-acetylene welding and cutting gear and a petrol-driven compressor to operate air tools. There was also a 7¹/₂-ton Gar Wood Industries' winch mounted behind the front bumper, and driven from the gearbox. This unit was intended solely for vehicle self-recovery.

Early models were issued with a set of top hoops and a canvas cover, which could be fitted to disguise the vehicle as a standard cargo truck from the air, but this was soon abandoned since it slowed down deployment of the recovery equipment. About 25% of production was fitted with a ring mount above the passenger seat,

intended for a .50in calibre M2 anti-aircraft machine gun; the M32 mount was fitted to closed-cab vehicles, and the M36 to open cabs.

The vehicle remained in production throughout the war, and the total number produced amounted to 6,240. It proved to be surprisingly durable, and remained classified as 'standard' by the US Army until 1953.

Diamond T Model 980/981, 45-ton tractor

The Diamond T Model 980/981, also known by US forces as the M20, formed the tractor component of the US Army's M19 45-ton tank-transporter train.

Originally developed at the behest of the British Truck Purchasing Commission in response to a requirement for a heavy tractor to supplement inadequate numbers of Scammell Pioneer tank transporters, the Model 980/981 was produced under the direction of the US Quartermaster Corps. The truck first appeared in 1941, remaining in production until 1945, by which time some 6,500 examples had been built. Although classified as 'substitute standard' by the US Army, it was widely used by all of the Allies and was considered a powerful and reliable truck, which could, in an emergency, operate on hard-surfaced roads at gross train weights approaching 72 tons (73,156kg).

Based on Diamond T's commercial 12-ton Model 512, from which it borrowed the same stylish art-deco 'de-luxe' cab as was fitted to the same manufacturer's 4-ton chassis, the M20 featured a long coffin nose which resulted in a surprisingly handsome appearance. Sadly, the stylish art-deco cab was abandoned in August 1943 in favour of a standardised open-cab design with a canvas top and flat, folding windscreen.

At the rear there was a simple steel ballast box, which allowed the truck to carry sufficient weight to provide adequate traction for the rear wheels when hitched to an overloaded three-axle 40 to 45-ton trailer.

Power was provided by a 14,500cc Hercules DFXE diesel engine; the use of

Above: Diamond T Model 981, the very similar Model 980 was not fitted with the winch fairlead in the front bumper. *(ST)*

Above: The Dodge ³/₄-ton Command Car (WC56-58) and the Carryall (WC53), shown, were often used as convoy lead vehicles in place of the more usual Jeep. *(DD)*

Right: Although not commonly used on the Red Ball or other supply routes, the ³/₄-ton Dodge weapons carrier (WC51, WC52) was widely used by truck maintenance companies for carrying tools and spare parts. *(PW)*

Above: Diamond T Model 980/981 showing just how much ammunition can be stacked onto the converted drawbar trailer. *(NA)*

diesel trucks was rare in the US Army during the war but this power unit was chosen in order to provide commonality of fuel with the Gardner 6LW-powered Scammells which were already in use by the British for the tank-transporter role. The engine produced 178bhp, combined with enormous torque, and drove double-reduction axles in the rear bogie through a twin-plate clutch, four-speed main gearbox and three-speed auxiliary gearbox.

The difference between the two models was minor; the Model 980 had no provision for winching from the front, whilst the Model 981, which appeared in 1942/43, incorporated fairlead rollers in the front bumper which allowed it to be used for tank recovery work as well as providing a self-recovery capability. In both cases, a 20-ton Gar Wood winch was fitted between the cab and ballast box.

Although it was originally intended as a prime mover for tank transporter trains,

at least two heavy truck companies on the Red Ball Express were equipped with M19 outfits which had been converted to act as load carriers. The twin trackways of the standard Rogers 45-ton M9 drawbar trailer - similar trailers were also supplied by Fruehauf, Winter Weiss, and Pointer-Williamette - were infilled using steel airfield track, and the same material was possibly used to construct fixed trailer sides. This allowed the trailer to carry 16.5 tons (16,765kg) of general supplies, 36 tons (36,579kg) of ammunition, 10 tons (10,160.5kg) of POL or 500 Jerrycans - at the time, this represented a very considerable lift. Similar vehicles were also converted to this role by British and Canadian units.

Federal 94X43, 4 to 5 ton tractor

Aside from its rounded nose and detail differences in the steering linkage, the Federal 94X43 was almost identical to

the Autocar U-7144T, and was intended for use with the same types of 10 and 12-ton (gross) weight semi-trailers. Mechanically, it was powered by the same type of Hercules engine, driving both axles through the same five-speed gearbox, with overdrive top gear and two-speed transfer case; the front axle could be disengaged when not required. The vehicle also shared a number of chassis components with the Autocar.

Live axles were hung on semi-elliptical leaf springs and the 20in (51cm) wheels were shod with 9.00x20 tyres, twinned at the rear. The brakes were air-pressure operated and there were four air-line connections for the semi-trailer brakes; a hand-control valve was fitted on the steering column to allow the semi-trailer brakes to be independently operated.

Early production examples (94X43A) were fitted with the standard Federal commercial two-door cab, combined with a short bonnet and a slightly rounded nose. Later models (94X43B and C)

received the typical military open cab which was used on virtually all US military trucks around 1942/43 with its soft top and folding windscreen. A tread-plate platform was fitted across the chassis rails ahead of the fifth wheel, and twin spare-wheel carriers were fitted behind the cab. One vehicle in four off the production line was fitted with an anti-aircraft gun mount; the M36 mount was used on open-cab vehicles and the M60 or M61 on closed cabs.

A total of 8,119 examples were produced between 1941 and 1945.

Trailers

A standard US Army fifth wheel was fitted, and typical semi-trailers used with this tractor on the Red Ball operation included:

- 5-ton (10 ton gross) refrigerator semi-trailer

- 6-ton 2,000 gallon (7,600 litre) fuel semi-trailer
- 6-ton (10 ton gross) van semi-trailer
- 7-ton (10 ton gross) cargo semi-trailer (G-596)
- 25ft (7.6m) wrecking semi-trailer, Type C-2
- $12^{1}/_{2}$-ton 40ft (12.2m) wrecking semi-trailer, Type C-2

Ford/Willys Jeep, $^{1}/_{4}$ ton truck

When it appeared in late 1940, the Jeep was a wholly-new type of military vehicle... an all-wheel drive $^{1}/_{4}$ ton utility truck which could replace the motorcycle, carry personnel and light cargo, perform reconnaissance roles and tow a light gun. It was hugely successful and, after the War, went on to spawn a hundred imitators.

Although the outline of the vehicle had been sketched out by the US Quartermaster Corps (QMC), the Jeep was effectively designed by freelance automotive designer Karl K. Probst working for the American Bantam Car Company over a long weekend in mid-1940. Despite the QMC having approached some 140 US motor manufacturers, American Bantam and Willys-Overland were the only companies to show any interest in the project and neither would have been the QMC's first choice. Bantam's prototype was delivered to the Army in September 1940, the Willys model followed soon after, but not before Willys' engineers had been allowed sight of the Bantam vehicle. High-level 'persuasion' also ensured that Ford submitted a prototype.

All three prototypes were tested at Camp Holabird in Maryland, and there followed a three-horse race for the production contracts.

Each design had its own strengths and weaknesses and the QMC found it difficult to choose between them so, initially, orders were placed with all three

Above and left:
A $2^{1}/_{2}$-ton GMC equipped with 750-gallon (2,839 litre) fuel tanks as issued to a light truck company. The chassis and automotive equipment were identical to the cargo vehicle. *(PW)*

Right: The volume of military traffic frequently turned the rich Normandy farm tracks into impassable mud. Here, the lone occupant of a Jeep, equipped for signals laying and up to its axles in mud, waits patiently as the driver of a GMC truck struggles to get the vehicle in position to effect a rescue. *(IWM/USE)*

Above and right:
The ³/₄-ton Dodge WC51.
The so-called weapons
carrier was widely used by
all units of the US Army.
The WC52 was equipped
with a winch but was
otherwise identical. *(PW)*

companies for 1500 vehicles each. By July 1941, the design had been standardised and Bantam was deemed too small to continue to have any role in the project. Ford and Willys went on to supply a total of 639,245 virtually-identical Jeeps between 1941 and 1945; the Willys model, which was known as the MB, was the most numerous with 361,349 examples built, whilst Ford constructed 277,896 examples of the GPW.

Differences between the two machines were minor and all parts were interchangeable. Both were powered by the 2,199cc Willys-designed Go-Devil, a long-stroke side-valve petrol engine, driving all four wheels through a Warner three-speed gearbox and Spicer two-speed transfer case; the front axle could be disengaged when not required. Aside

from the provision of steering gear, identical Spicer live axles were used at front and rear, suspended on semi-elliptical multi-leaf springs; brakes were hydraulic, without power assistance; and the truck ran on 6.00x16 tyres mounted on two-piece steel rims.

The vehicle's body was little more than an open steel tub with flat-topped front mudguards and a simple curved bonnet. The windscreen could be folded flat to the bonnet to reduce the vehicle's profile. There were small seats for four men, with the rear seat able to be folded upwards to provide a small cargo area. A crude canvas top was all that most vehicles were fitted with in terms of weather equipment although canvas doors and side-screens became available.

Above: The Dodge WC53 Carryall is one of the more unusual variants of the ³/₄-ton WC series and might have been used as a convoy lead vehicle on any of the supply routes. A total of 8,400 were built between 1942 and 1943. *(ST)*

Above: Although the Allies enjoyed virtual air superiority in the weeks following D-Day, anti-aircraft support was generally still provided in every convoy. A percentage of the trucks were fitted with a ring-mounted .50in-calibre machine gun, but many convoys were accompanied by trucks equipped with four .50in-calibre machine guns in a Maxson M2 electrically-operated mount. Each gun had a maximum rate of fire of 450 rounds per minute. *(ST)*

The Jeep proved to be incredibly versatile and, aside from intended roles, the vehicle was used in service as a front-line ambulance, for communications, machine gun mount, anti-tank vehicle, line layer, railway shunter and desert patrol vehicle. On the Red Ball Express, Jeeps were used by Convoy Commanders and also by the Military Police.

Ford also built an amphibious version known as the GPA.

GMC AFKWX, 2¹/₂-ton truck

The GMC AFKWX was basically a forward-control (cab over engine, COE) commercial truck which had been modified for military service by the addition of a driven front axle. Production started in 1942 and, initially, the truck shared the same commercial two-man Chevrolet cab design as the CCKW. In this instance, it was mated to a short, rounded bonnet and full-width grille; a full-width metal brush guard was provided to protect the radiator. Later models (1944-45) used an open cab with a canvas top and flat, folding windscreen mated to the same bonnet design.

In theory, the vehicle was manufactured in long and short-wheelbase form, although only a handful of the latter were built, all in 1940, and were powered by the smaller Model 256 engine of 4,195cc. By far the majority of AFKWX production was of the long-wheelbase '353' designation and, although it was not produced in the same range of variants as the CCKW, there was a choice of 15ft (4.6m) and 17ft (5.2m) steel cargo bodies, the former fitted with troop seats; six removable hoops were provided to support a canvas cover. One out of four trucks off the production line was fitted with an M36 anti-aircraft machine gun mount.

The big advantage of the AFKWX over the more numerous CCKW lay in the extended length of the cargo bed,

when compared to the standard 12ft (3.7m), which was made possible by the forward-control cab layout.

All of the '353' models were powered by a 4,416cc Chevrolet Model 270 six-cylinder overhead-valve engine, driving all six wheels through a five-speed gearbox and two-speed transfer case; the driver could disengage the front axle when not required. The live axles were suspended on semi-elliptical multi-leaf springs; early axles, which were susceptible to catastrophic failure through over-loading, were of the Timken-Detroit 'split' type, the later GM-designed 'banjo' axles proving to be far more durable. Standard tyre size was 7.50x20 with dual tyres fitted at the rear. A modest 7,602 examples were constructed by the Yellow Truck & Coach Manufacturing Company, and the GMC Truck & Coach Division, between 1942 and 1945.

The model code 'AFKWX' indicates that the truck was designed in 1939 ('A'), was fitted with a forward-control cab,

('F'), front-wheel drive ('K'), rear-wheel bogie drive ('W'), and had a non-standard wheelbase ('X'); the numbers '352' and '353' indicate the wheelbase lengths but have no significance beyond that.

GMC CCKW, 2¹/₂-ton truck

Nicknamed the 'deuce-and-a-half' or the 'Jimmy', the GMC 2¹/₂-ton 6x6 was probably the most significant US truck of World War Two and, with some 562,750 produced, was the truck most commonly associated with the Red Ball Express. It was also the most numerous tactical vehicle of the war, beaten from the top spot only by the mighty Jeep.

GMC had started supplying lightly-militarised, but essentially-civilian, 2¹/₂-ton 4x2 and 6x6 trucks to the US Army from 1939, but the vehicle for which they became known worldwide was derived from the 2¹/₂-ton 6x6 normal-control ACKWX-353, not to be

Above: Far less numerous than the standard GMC CCKW was the, otherwise similar forward-control AFKWX. The vehicle was also produced with both open and closed cabs and in different wheelbase lengths. *(DD)*

confused with the forward-control AFKWX which came later. The ACKWX had also been intended for the French Army but supplies were diverted to Britain when France fell to the Germans in 1940.

In January 1941, the civilian front end of the ACKWX was replaced by a no-compromise and slightly ill-fitting military bonnet, radiator and front wings to produce the standardised, normal-control CCKW (initially designated 'CCKWX'); it was produced in two chassis lengths, the '353' having a wheelbase of 13ft 8in (4.12m), the '352' measuring 12ft (3.7m). The standard Chevrolet civilian cab of the earlier vehicle with its curious V-shaped top-hung screen, survived until 1944 when it was replaced by an open cab with a canvas top and flat, folding windscreen. Whilst most cargo bodies were of welded-steel construction, timber bodies were also fitted; both types had fixed sides and a drop tailgate, and included folding troop seats in the rear. Five removable hoops were provided to support a canvas cover.

The long-wheelbase cargo truck was the most numerous in production, but there was also a host of other variants, including a 750-gallon (2,850 litre) fuel tanker, 700-gallon (2,850 litre) water tanker, stake truck, compressor vehicle, workshop vehicle, bomb-service truck, dump truck (tipper), and van body; the truck was also supplied in chassis-cab form for the construction of specialised bodies. A percentage of vehicles were fitted with a Gar Wood or Heil 10,000 lb (4,545kg) capacity winch installed on chassis extensions ahead of the radiator, and one out of four trucks off the production line was fitted with an anti-aircraft machine-gun mount, either the M32 mount (closed cab, long-wheelbase),

M37 (closed or open cab, short-wheelbase), or M36 (open cab, long-wheelbase).

Like the AFKWX-353, all of these trucks were powered by a 4,416cc Chevrolet six-cylinder water-cooled overhead-valve petrol engine, driving all wheels through a five-speed gearbox and two-speed transfer case; the front axle could be disengaged when not required. Suspension was by semi-elliptical multi-leaf springs and there were two types of axle design, described as 'split' or 'banjo', the latter being less susceptible to catastrophic failure through over-loading. Standard tyre size was 7.50x20, with dual tyres fitted at the rear.

The Yellow Truck & Coach Manufacturing Company, and the General Motors Truck & Coach Division produced the vehicles. The model code 'CCKW' indicates that the truck was designed in 1941 (first 'C'), was fitted with a normal-control cab (second 'C'), front-wheel drive ('K') and rear-wheel bogie drive ('W'); the 'X' suffix, which indicated a non-standard wheelbase, was dropped soon after manufacture began. The numbers '352' and '353' indicate the wheelbase lengths but have no other significance.

Although the prototype amphibious DUKW was based on the AFKWX-353, automotive components from the CCKW were used to produce some 21,000 production DUKWs... hundreds of which were used to bring supplies ashore at the Normandy beachheads before full-scale harbour facilities were available.

Trailers

The CCKW was often coupled to a 1-ton two-wheeled steel cargo trailer (G-518), typically produced by Ben Hur Manufacturing Company.

Left: GMC CCKW and
Ward LaFrance or
Kenworth M1A1 heavy
wrecker. The M1A1 was
the standard heavy
recovery vehicle of the
US Army and many were
deployed on the Red Ball
and other supply routes.
(PR)

Above and right:
Restored GMCs on parade.
(PR)

Above: The 1½-ton Chevrolet cargo truck was not used on the European supply routes, but the tractor version was used in conjunction with a range of 6-ton (gross) trailers. *(PR)*

Left: Nice open-cab GMC with the tarpaulin pulled back to show the stakes which were used to extend the height of the body sides. This vehicle is also equipped with an anti-aircraft machine gun. *(PR)*

Above: A US Army multiple gun motor carriage (MGMC) M16. Note the ammunition drums are not fitted. *(ST)*

Right: The MGMC M16 carried four .50in-calibre M2 machine guns in a Maxson mount. *(ST)*

Harley-Davidson WLA motorcycle

The military motorcycle that Harley-Davidson started to build for the US Army in 1939, and continued to build until 1944, was designated the 40-WLA - the 'A' suffix indicating that it was an 'army' or military model. As modifications were made, it became the 41-WLA and 42-WLA.

It was actually little more than a heavy-duty, militarised version of the company's hard-tail DLD civilian 'sports special solo' model the origins of which could be traced back to the late 1920s. The 737cc V-twin civilian 'WL' side-valve engine was down-rated by reducing the compression ratio to 5:1. The engine had larger than standard cooling fins to help cope with overheating when used off-road. Additional military fittings included a lower chain guard, engine skid plate, crash bars, large air cleaner, luggage rack with leather pannier bags, rifle scabbard and ammunition stowage.

The engine drove via a foot-operated multi-disc oil bath-type clutch to a three-speed gearbox operated by a hand-change. The front forks were of the parallelogram girder design typical of the period and fitted with twin coil-spring suspension. Rear suspension was 'solid', relying on a softly-sprung generous-shaped leather saddle to cushion the rider from road shocks.

The WL rode on large, 18in (46cm), wheels fitted with 4.00 or 4.50 tyres, with wide-section mudguards provided to prevent build-up of mud. Plenty of torque was available from the engine for the rough conditions but unfortunately, poor ground clearance - little more than 4in (10cm) - militated against arduous off-road riding. On the road, the big Harley was capable of almost 60mph (97kph) - good considering it weighed around 650lb (294kg) - and was extremely reliable, making it the perfect choice for reconnaissance operations for the

Above: A US Army M1 Bofors 90mm anti-aircraft gun. Units such as this were positioned beside transport routes or travelled with the convoys. *(JSS)*

US Military Police and dispatch rider services. In the latter roles it was deployed on the Red Ball Express.

In all, around 89,000 examples were manufactured between 1940 and Spring 1944 - 60,000 of these went to the US forces, the remainder being supplied to the various Allies, including Great Britain, Australia, Canada, China and the USSR. There was also a Canadian-built model, designated WLC, which differed in detail.

IHC M425, M426, 5-ton tractor

In 1943, the US Ordnance Department proposed the introduction of two new 4x2 tractor units for long-distance road work by the Transportation and Ordnance Corps. Both were described as 5-ton tractors. The H-542-9 was intended for use with a 5-ton (10-ton gross), 16ft (4.9m) semi-trailer, and was eventually designated

M425, whilst the heavier H-542-11, eventually known as M426, was to be used with a 5-ton (10-ton gross), 25ft (7.6m) semi-trailer. The differences between the two vehicles were not at all obvious, being confined to such small items as the number of leaves in the springs of the rear suspension and the tyre size.

Both were built as prototypes and then manufactured by International Harvester Company (IHC) in early 1944, with the 'light' M425 eventually being abandoned. Additional production capacity for the M426 was subsequently provided by the Marmon-Herrington and Kenworth companies who built identical vehicles. Many of the M425s produced were subsequently converted to M426 specification.

Regardless of manufacturer, all these vehicles were powered by the same type of 7,390cc IHC Red Diamond

six-cylinder water-cooled petrol engine, driving the single rear axle through a five-speed gearbox; a Timken double-reduction axle was used at the rear.

The suspension was carried on semi-elliptical leaf springs. Brakes were air-pressure operated with four air-line connections to the semi-trailer brakes; a hand-control valve was fitted inside the vehicle to allow the semi-trailer brakes to be operated independently. Wheels were 20in (51cm) diameter and were fitted with 9.00x20 or 11.00x20 tyres, depending on the weight classification.

The truck was of the semi-forward control layout with a short stubby bonnet and wide radiator grille giving way to a simple tub-type open cab produced by Hayes Manufacturing. The flat windscreen could be folded down onto the bonnet. A removable canvas top and side-screens for weather protection

was fitted. An M36 anti-aircraft gun mount could be mounted on the cab.

A total of 15,618 were manufactured between 1943 and 1945; 4,640 of the M425 variant were produced by IHC; with 10,978 of the heavier M426 from IHC (6,678), Marmon-Herrington (3,200) and Kenworth (1,100).

Trailers

A standard US Army fifth wheel was fitted, and typical semi-trailers used with this tractor on the Red Ball operation included:

- 5-ton (10-ton gross) refrigerator semi-trailer
- 6-ton 2,000-gallon (7,600 litre) fuel semi-trailer
- 6-ton (10-ton gross) van semi-trailer
- 7-ton (10-ton gross) cargo semi-trailer (G-596)

Right: Every supply route convoy included vehicles equipped with machine guns for anti-aircraft defence. Half-tracked and Dodge gun motor carriages were also mixed in with the convoys. *(PR)*

TC ★ TRK44

Above: The convoy lead vehicle was always marked accordingly. This GMC 6x6 is towing an armoured ammunition trailer. *(PR)*

- 25ft (7.6m) wrecking semi-trailer, Type C-2
- 12.5-ton 40ft (12m) wrecking semi-trailer, Type C-2

Studebaker US6, 2½-ton tractor

Although GMC is best known as the major producer of 2½-ton trucks for the US Army during World War Two, similar vehicles were also supplied by International and Studebaker.

Similar in appearance to the GMC, Studebaker's contribution was designated as the US6 Series, with different suffixes assigned to each variant, and was produced in both 6x6 and 6x4 form, and in long and short-wheelbase configurations. The short-wheelbase 6x4 chassis was used by the US

Army as a 2½-ton tractor for semi-trailers, and many were operated on the Red Ball Express route. The 6x4 was virtually identical to the 6x6 but with the driven front axle omitted, which greatly simplified spares inventory.

Power was provided by a 5,245cc Hercules JXD side-valve six-cylinder water-cooled petrol engine, driving either the rear four, or all wheels, through a five-speed gearbox with an overdrive top gear, and single-speed transfer case. Late production vehicles were fitted with a two-speed transfer case and, as standard, the front axle on 6x6 variants could be disengaged. The axles were suspended on semi-elliptical leaf springs, inverted at the rear. The vehicle's brakes were hydraulic with vacuum servo assistance.

chassis was also used as a cargo truck (US6x4-U7 and U8).

Most of these vehicles were supplied to the Allies, particularly Great Britain, Australia and the USSR as part of the Lend-Lease program but small numbers of the tractors were used on the Red Ball Express.

Trailers

A standard US Army fifth wheel was fitted, and typical semi-trailers used with this tractor on the Red Ball operation included:

- 5-ton (10-ton gross) refrigerator semi-trailer
- 6-ton (10-ton gross) van semi-trailer
- 7-ton (10-ton gross) cargo semi-trailer (G-596)

Ward LaFrance Model 1000, 6-ton wrecker

The design of the US Army's heavy recovery vehicle was standardised in 1937 as 'truck, wrecking, heavy, M1'. The vehicle, which was built by both Ward LaFrance and Kenworth, was intended for towing, salvaging and recovery operations of wheeled and light tracked vehicles. The M1 was also equipped to carry out repair operations away from base workshops using heavy hoisting and winching equipment.

Ward LaFrance used a 10-ton (later downgraded to 6-ton) Model 1000 6x6 series 1 chassis as the basis for the M1, with production vehicles first appearing in 1941. The Kenworth Model 570 followed soon after. The two vehicles were very similar in design and appearance. Both were fitted with the 8,210cc Continental 22R dual-ignition petrol engine, Fuller transmission and Timken drive-line. A Gar Wood hand-

It is ironic that although Studebaker developed the US Army's standard open-cab design, most of the company's US6 trucks were fitted with a civilian-type commercial cab with a typically-ungainly military front end. The flat curved mudguards and an upright radiator guard were not unlike those used on the GMC. Of the vast number built, only 10,000 examples were fitted with an open cab.

Production of the US6 started in June 1941 and continued until August 1945 by which time 197,678 examples of all models had been manufactured. A further 22,204 identical trucks were also produced by Reo Motors Inc (the US6-U3 variant, with a cargo body). Of the total production, 82,104 trucks were fitted with a 6x4 drive-line and identified as US6x4, the tractor-unit version being designated US6x4-U6. The 6x4

Right: The 4-ton Diamond T Model 969 was the standard medium recovery truck, or wrecker, of the US Army, and was widely used on supply line road patrol duties. *(TM)*

operated crane was standard equipment. Minor modifications saw the introduction of the Ward LaFrance Model 1000 Series 2, 3 and 4, and the Kenworth Model 572, before production was halted and concentrated on the standardised M1A1.

By this time, some 2,030 examples of the M1 had been constructed, the largest number from Ward LaFrance.

The M1A1 appeared in 1943. It had improved lifting equipment and was fitted with an open cab which had an uncompromisingly-utilitarian appearance. Again, the truck was manufactured by both Ward LaFrance and Kenworth, both companies producing what was effectively the same vehicle. A total of 3,735 M1A1s were produced between 1943 and 1945, with Ward LaFrance responsible for the majority.

Ward LaFrance used the same 6x6 heavy-duty truck chassis as had been developed for the M1 wrecker, now designating it Series 5; Kenworth's chassis

was described as the Model 573. Differences between the two vehicles amounted to little more than the shape of the whiffle tree and the side-mounted tool lockers.

Both manufacturers fitted a front-mounted 8,210cc Continental 22R six-cylinder water-cooled petrol engine and drive was through a dry clutch to a five-speed gearbox, a remote-mounted two-speed transfer case, then Timken axles at front and rear. Drive to the front axle could be disengaged when not required. Top speed on the road was 45mph (72kph) and the vehicle had excellent cross-country performance.

Suspension was by conventional multi-leaf semi-elliptical springs, inverted at the rear, where the axle was located by radius rods. Hydraulic shock absorbers were fitted to the front axle. Brakes were air operated with brake line connections at front and rear. A double-check valve in the brake lines allowed the vehicle to be braked by a towing vehicle.

The introduction of the M1A1 saw the earlier closed cab design changed to a narrow, open cab of the typical tub design adopted for virtually all US military trucks in the latter years of the war. The cab provided seating for two crew members; the canvas top could be removed and side curtains/doors were available to provide a winter enclosure. The windscreen could be folded flat on the bonnet. Twin spare wheels were carried alongside the crane mast. Top hoops and a tarpaulin were carried to camouflage the vehicle as a cargo truck from the air. These vehicles were frequently fitted with the M2 anti-aircraft ring mount.

The Gar Wood manual crane on the M1 was replaced by a fully-powered unit, which could be slewed through 180° to lift at the rear or side of the vehicle. Lifting capacity varied according to the elevation of the sliding jib and the position of the jib hook line. Maximum lifting capacity was 16,000lb (7,258kg). Jacks were provided at each side

and rear to support the vehicle during lifting operations. Drum-type Gar Wood powered winches were fitted at front and rear – the rear unit had a capacity of 37,500lb (17,010kg), and was designed for straight or angled recovery. The front winch had a 20,000lb (9,072kg) capacity and was intended primarily for vehicle self-recovery.

Welding and cutting equipment was carried, with three gas bottles in a rack behind the cab; a considerable amount of tools and other equipment was stowed in various lockers.

Production began in 1943 at the Kenworth plant in Seattle (later moved to Yakima, Washington State in 1944) and at the Ward LaFrance factory at Elmira, New York. In 1945, Kenworth was purchased by Pacific Car & Foundry and production was moved back to Seattle.

The new design was not standardised until March 1944 which meant that more than a few M1A1s were produced with the incorrect designation 'M1'.

Above: The Continental-engined M1A1 heavy wrecker was built by both Kenworth and Ward LaFrance in almost identical form. The Gar Wood 5-ton capacity swinging-boom crane allowed the vehicle to work to the side or the rear. A total of 3,735 were built between 1943 and 1945. *(PW)*

Right: Diamond T Model 969 wrecker being used to recover a 2$^1/_2$-ton GMC. Equipped with a Holmes twin-boom crane, the Diamond T was an extremely versatile vehicle. The two booms could be used separately or combined allowing a total pull of 10 tons. *(TM)*

6 | Lies, Damned Lies and Statistics

The Red Ball Express ran for a total of 84 days. During that time, 412,243 tons (418,839 tonnes) of supplies were moved. Subsequent operations moved more than another 1,250,000 tons (1,270,000 tonnes) of supplies. The largest of these, the XYZ Express ran for 68 days and shifted 871,895 tons (885,845 tonnes) of supplies.

Right: Following the breakout from the Cotentin Peninsula, the US First and Third Armies required 600,000 gallons (2,280,00 litres) of fuel a day. By late August, the two armies were consuming something like 1,500,000 gallons (5,700,000 litres) a day, and the daily fuel requirement for the Red Ball trucks alone was estimated at 300,000 gallons (1,140,000 litres). *(PR)*

Authors note: All figures are quoted from US military sources. In most cases the individual figures have come from several different sources and the items listed may not necessarily agree or cross-check; the figure for ton-miles for example has been taken from official sources and has not been calculated from the total tonnage and mileage figures quoted.

RED BALL EXPRESS

Red Ball Express 'Phase One'

Purpose: to support US First and Third Armies in the advance across France and towards Germany

Route: St Lô to Dreux/Chartres area
Operation commenced: 25 August 1944
Operation terminated: 5 September 1944
Number of operational days: 12
Average daily haul: 8,885 tons (9,027 tonnes)
Total tonnage: 88,939 tons (90,362 tonnes)
Average round trip: 308 miles (496km)
Total (loaded) ton-miles: 9,783,290
Maximum number of truck companies involved: 132
Average number of truck companies involved: 83
Approximate number of trucks involved: 5,958

Red Ball Express 'Phase Two'

Purpose: to support US First and Third Armies in the advance across France and towards Germany

Route: St Lô to Paris, Soissons and Sommesous
Operation commenced: 6 September 1944
Operation terminated: 16 November 1944
Number of operational days: 72
Average daily haul: 4,552 tons (4,625 tonnes)
Total tonnage: 323,304 tons (328,477 tonnes)
Average round trip: 320 miles (515km)
Total (loaded) ton-miles: 51,728,640
Maximum number of truck companies involved: 133
Average number of truck companies involved: 74
Approximate number of trucks involved: 5,178

Above: The statue of the Emperor Napoleon III in Cherbourg harbour stands over the scene of 2$^1/_2$-ton GMC trucks being loaded. *(PW)*

Right: Similar to the Autocar U-7144T, the Federal 94X43 was also a 4-5 ton tractor intended for use with semi-trailers. Although it was powered by the same Hercules engine as the Autocar, it can be readily identified by its more rounded nose. Like the Autocar the vehicle was also produced with open and closed cabs. *(DD)*

Red Ball Express in total

Purpose: to support US First and Third Armies in the advance across France and towards Germany

Route: St Lô to Dreux/Chartres area, Paris, Soissons, and Sommesous
Operation commenced: 25 August 1944
Operation terminated: 16 November 1944
Number of operational days: 84
Average daily haul: 4,908 tons (4,986 tonnes)
Total tonnage: 412,243 tons (418,839 tonnes)
Average round trip: 555 miles (893km)
Total (loaded) ton-miles: 112,336,218
Maximum number of truck companies involved: 133
Average number of truck companies involved: 83
Approximate number of trucks involved: 5,400

OTHER EXPRESS TRUCK ROUTES

Red Lion Express

Purpose: to support British/Canadian 21st Army Group on 'Operation Market Garden'

Route: Bayeux to Brussels
Operation commenced: 13 September 1944
Operation terminated: 12 October 1944
Number of operational days: 30
Average daily haul: 627 tons (637 tonnes)
Total tonnage: 17,556 tons (17,837 tonnes)
Average round trip: 720 miles (1,159km)
Total (loaded) ton-miles: 6,320,160
Maximum number of truck companies involved: 9
Average number of truck companies involved: 8

Above: Three International 4x2 tractors coupled to the C2 wrecking semi-trailer. Although primarily designed for transporting salvaged and new aircraft, this trailer, which had a 12$\frac{1}{2}$-ton payload, was also occasionally used for what the US Army described as 'general purpose hauling'. *(TM)*

153

Approximate number of trucks involved: 246

White Ball Express

Purpose: to clear the ports of Le Havre and Rouen by transferring supplies to the railheads at Paris, Beauvais and Compeigne
Route: Le Havre to Rouen and Paris; Rouen to Rheims; Rouen to Beauvais

Operation commenced: 6 October 1944
Operation terminated: 6 January 1945
Number of operational days: 93
Average daily haul: 1,473 tons (1,497 tonnes)
Total tonnage: 143,067 tons (145,356 tonnes)
Average round trip: 225 miles (362 km)
Total (loaded) ton-miles: 16,166,751
Maximum number of truck companies

Left: A column of 1½-ton Chevrolet 4x4 tractors coupled to the 3½-ton (6 ton gross) stake and platform semi-trailer. The trucks are being refuelled from the inevitable Jerrycans. The legend on the windscreen of the lead vehicle, which has not been completely obliterated by the censor, suggests that the trucks are intended to haul ammunition. *(FC)*

involved: 48
Average number of truck companies involved: 29
Approximate number of trucks involved: 928

Green Diamond Express

Purpose: to move supplies from the Normandy depots to railheads at Avranches and Dol-de-Bretagne

Route: Normandy to Avranches and Dol-de-Bretagne
Operation commenced: 10 October 1944
Operation terminated: 1 November 1944
Number of operational days: 23
Average daily haul: 1,473 tons (1,497 tonnes)
Total tonnage: 15,590 tons (15,839 tonnes)

Above: GMC trucks being loaded with Jerrycans. The vehicles were permitted to be overloaded by 100% which means that a GMC was capable of carrying 250 cans of fuel amounting to 1,100 gallons (5,001 litre). Some contemporary photographs suggest that it was possible to carry 360 cans in three layers of 120 each. *(PW)*

Average round trip: 200 miles (322km)
Total (loaded) ton-miles: 15,59,900
Maximum number of truck companies involved: 19
Average number of truck companies involved: 15
Approximate number of trucks involved: 600

ABC Express

Purpose: to clear the port of Antwerp, moving supplies in support of US First and Ninth Armies and the British/Canadian 21st Army Group in the drive across northwest Europe

Route: Antwerp to Brussels, Liege, Charleroi and Mons
Operation commenced: 30 November 1944
Operation terminated: 26 March 1945
Number of operational days: 117
Average daily haul: 2,092 tons (2,126 tonnes)
Average round trip: 200 miles (322km)
Total tonnage: 244,924 tons (248,843 tonnes)
Total (loaded) ton-miles: 24,492,000
Maximum number of truck companies involved: 14
Average number of truck companies involved: 14

Approximate number of trucks involved: 560

Little Red Ball

Purpose: to move 100 tons of supplies a day from Cherbourg to Paris

Route: Cherbourg to Paris
Operation commenced: 15 December 1944
Operation terminated: 17 January 1945
Number of operational days: 34
Average daily haul: 106 tons (108 tonnes)
Total tonnage: 3,507 tons (3,563 tonnes)
Average round trip: 350 miles (563km)
Total (loaded) ton-miles: 613,725

Maximum number of truck companies involved: 1
Average number of truck companies involved: 1
Approximate number of trucks involved: 48

XYZ Express

Purpose: to support US First, Third, Seventh and Ninth Armies during the final push into Germany

Route: Liege, Duren, Luxembourg and Nancy into Germany
Operation commenced: 25 March 1945
Operation terminated: 31 May 1945

Above: Every loaded truck which particpated in any supply run carried spare fuel in every available space and Jerrycans became one of the basic needs of the advance. Empty cans were gathered up and returned to the fuel depots all over the Normandy area for refilling. Empty cans were stacked flat, whilst full cans were stood upright to prevent leakage from the cap. *(IWM/USE)*

Left: Tyres came in for a particular beating due to factors such as under-inflation, over-loading, excessive speed, bad road surfaces and general bad driving. Until January 1945, Ordnance had just one operational tyre repair company, the 158th, of which just two out of six teams were assigned to ADSEC. *(IWM/USE)*

Far left: Thousands of GMCs were left in Europe at the end of the war, and more than 7,500 were still in use with the French Army some 30 years later which probably accounts for the popularity of the truck with collectors. Note the *Wehrmacht*-marked barrel in the left-hand photograph: *Kraftstoff* translates simply as 'fuel'. *(PW)*

Number of operational days: 68
Average daily haul: 12,895 tons (13,101 tonnes)
Total tonnage: 871,895 tons (885,845 tonnes) (630,000 tons [640,080 tonnes] by VE Day, 8 May 1945)
Average round trip: 250 miles (402km)
Total (loaded) ton-miles: 111,710,479

Maximum number of truck companies involved: 120 (initial plans called for 55 under 'Plan X'; 67 under 'Plan Y'; and 81 under 'Plan Z')
Average number of truck companies involved: 80
Approximate number of trucks involved: 4,800

Left: A convoy of US Army fuel tankers halts at a checkpoint in France, 15 September 1944. *(NA)*

Far left: Perhaps the most famous Red Ball photograph of all. Taken near Alençon, France, 5 September 1944. It shows Corporal Charles H. Johnson of the 783rd Military Police Battalion directing a Red Ball convoy. *(NA)*

Left: Although they were similar in appearance, the US-designed Jerrycans differed from those produced by the British and Germans and, with their screw necks, were more prone to leakage. With their prominent centre seam, the cans in this stack are mostly British or German. The fourth can in the third row shows the distinctive screw neck which was a feature of the US-type Jerrycan. *(IWM/USE)*

Left: Beef carcasses being offloaded in Batilly, France, 30 September 1944, from (unrefrigerated) 2¹/₂-ton GMC trucks and put into the back of a rather battered Dodge WC51 weapons carrier. Combat troops did not always receive fresh food and there is a story that says that the US Seventh Army exchanged two truck loads of Nazi souvenirs with the Third Army, in return receiving two truck loads of food. The exchange took place at a Red Ball depot. *(NA)*

LIGHT
VEHICLE
REFUELIN
POINT

Left: Fuel from a GMC tanker is discharged into the underground tanks of a civilian service station which has been comandeered to provide a refueling point for light vehicles. *(FC)*

Above: Preserved GMCs lined up at a re-enactment of a Red Ball depot. *(MB)*

Far left: Although the setting is certainly France, the MP is obviously British and the truck is a Studebaker US6 rather than the ubiquitous GMC. This photograph serves as a reminder that the British Army faced similar supply problems during the advance even if the solutions were less glamorous. *(IWM)*

Left: A multiple gun motor carriage (MGMC) M16 with 'in the field' applied winter camouflage. Vehicles such as this sometimes travelled with the convoys to provide air cover. *(TM)*

Appendix: Vehicle Specifications

Autocar U-7144T, 4 to 5 ton tractor

Typical nomenclature: truck, 4 to 5 ton, 4x4, tractor; Autocar U-7144T, White 444T.
Manufacturer: Autocar Company, Ardmore, Pennsylvania. The White Motor Company, Cleveland, Ohio.
Standard Nomenclature List: G-510, G-691.
Classification: standard.

Specification
Engine: 8,669cc Hercules RXC-529; six-cylinder water-cooled side-valve petrol engine; net power output, 112bhp at 2,200rpm; maximum torque, 395 lbf/ft at 1,000rpm.
Transmission: 5F1Rx2; over-drive top gear; part-time 4x4.
Suspension: live axles on multi-leaf semi-elliptical springs.
Brakes: air pressure; drums all-round; four trailer air-line connections.
Construction: channel-section steel ladder chassis; pressed-steel welded cab.
Electrical system: dual 6-12V.

Dimensions
Length: 17ft (5.2m). **Width,** 7ft 11in (2.41m). **Height,** (open cab, top in place) 9ft 5in (2.87m); (reduced) 7ft 8in (2.34m).
Wheelbase: 11ft 3in (3.43m).
Ground clearance: 11.75in (30cm).
Payload: 9,350lb (4,241.2kg).
Weight: (unladen) 11,606lb (5,264.5kg); (loaded) 21,000lb (9,525kg).
Normal towed load: 20,000lb (9,072kg).

Performance
Maximum allowable speed: 41mph (66kph).
Average fuel consumption: 3.5mpg (1.24km/litre).
Range of action: 180 to 200 miles (174 to 322km).
Approach angle: 54°; departure angle, 50°.

Above and right:
The 4 to 5 ton tractor was powered by a 8,669cc Hercules RXC six-cylinder water-cooled side-valve petrol engine driving both axles through a five-speed gearbox. *(DD)*

Chevrolet G-4113, G-7113, 1¹/₂ ton tractor

Typical nomenclature: truck, 1¹/₂ ton, 4x4, tractor; Chevrolet Type G-4113, G-7113.
Manufacturer: Chevrolet Motor Division, General Motors Corporation, Detroit, Michigan.
Standard Nomenclature List: G-506.
Classification: standard.

Specification
Engine: 3,859cc Chevrolet BV1001-UP; six-cylinder water-cooled overhead-valve petrol engine; net power output, 84bhp at 3,000rpm; maximum torque, 189 lbf/ft at 1,600rpm.
Transmission: 4F1Rx2; part-time 4x4.
Suspension: live axles on multi-leaf semi-elliptical springs.
Brakes: hydraulic, with Hydrovac vacuum servo assistance; drums all-round; electric connection for trailer brakes.
Construction: channel-section steel ladder chassis; pressed-steel welded cab.
Electrical system: 6V.

Dimensions
Length: 17ft 2in (5.2m). **Width,** 7ft 2in (2.2m). **Height,** 7ft 3in (2.21m).
Wheelbase: 12ft 1in (3.7m).
Ground clearance: 9.88in (25.1cm).

Above: The 1¹/₂ ton Chevrolet tractor was originally intended for use in the Far East but was pressed into service on the Red Ball route due to a lack of other suitable vehicles. *(DD)*

Payload: 4,820lb (2,186.4kg).
Weight: (unladen) 6,045lb (2,742kg); (gross) 10,865lb (4,928.4kg).
Normal towed load: 12,000lb (5,443kg).

Performance
Maximum allowable speed: 48mph (77kph).
Average fuel consumption: 9mpg (3.2km/litre).
Range of action: 270 miles (434.5km).
Approach angle: 45°; departure angle, 30°.

Diamond T Model 969, 4-ton wrecker

Typical nomenclature: truck, wrecker, 4 ton, 6x6; Diamond T Model 969, 969A, 969B.
Manufacturer: Diamond T Motor Car Company, Chicago, Illinois.
Standard Nomenclature List: G-509.
Classification: standard.

Specification
Engine: 8,669cc Hercules RXC-529; six-cylinder water-cooled side-valve petrol engine; net power output, 112bhp at 2,200rpm; maximum torque, 395 lbf/ft at 1,000rpm.
Transmission: 5F1Rx2; over-drive top gear; part-time 4x4.
Suspension: live axles on multi-leaf semi-elliptical springs, inverted at rear.
Brakes: air pressure; drums all-round; brake line connections at front and rear for towing.
Construction: channel-section steel ladder chassis; pressed-steel welded cab and body.
Electrical system: 12V.

Dimensions

Length: 24ft 4in (7.42m). **Width,** 7ft 10in (2.4m). **Height,** (to top of bracing structure) 9ft 3in (2.8m).
Wheelbase: 12ft 7in (3.84m).
Bogie centres: 4ft 4in (132cm).
Ground clearance: 11in (28cm).
Weight: (unladen) 19,500lb (8,845kg), (gross) 21,700lb (9,843kg).
Maximum towed load: 20,000lb (9,072kg).

Performance

Maximum allowable speed: 40mph (64kph).
Average fuel consumption: 3.5mpg (1.24km/litre).
Range of action: 180 miles (290km).
Approach angle: 37°; departure angle, 46°.

Diamond T Model 980/981, 45 ton tractor

Typical nomenclature: truck, 12 ton, 6x4, prime mover, M20; Diamond T Model 980, 981.
Manufacturer: Diamond T Motor Car Company, Chicago, Illinois.
Standard Nomenclature List: G-159.
Classification: substitute standard.

Specification

Engine: 14,500cc Hercules DFXE; six-cylinder water-cooled overhead-valve diesel engine; net power output, 178bhp at 1,800rpm; maximum torque, 685 lbf/ft at 1,150rpm.

Above: Similar to the Autocar U-7144T, the Federal 94x43 was also a 4 to 5 ton tractor intended for use with semi-trailers. Although it was powered by the same Hercules engine as the Autocar, it can be readily identified by its more rounded nose. Like the Autocar, the vehicle was also produced with open and closed cabs. *(DD)*

Transmission: 4F1Rx3; 6x4.

Suspension: live axles on multi-leaf semi-elliptical springs, inverted at rear.

Brakes: compressed air; drums all-round; two trailer air-line connections, at front and rear.

Construction: channel-section steel ladder chassis; pressed-steel welded cab; fabricated sheet-steel ballast box.

Electrical system: hybrid 24/12/6V.

Dimensions

Length: 23ft 4in (7.1m). **Width,** 8ft 5in (2.6m). **Height,** (closed cab) 8ft 5in (2.6m), (open cab) 8ft 10in (2.7m).

Wheelbase: 14ft 11in (4.55m).

Bogie centres: 4ft 4in (1.3m).

Ground clearance: 11in (28cm).

Weight: (unladen) 26,650lb (12,088kg); (gross, with trailer) 50,288lb (22,811kg).

Maximum towed load: 115,000lb (52,164 kg).

Gross train weight: 145,460lb (65,981kg).

Performance

Maximum allowable speed: 22mph (35kph).

Average fuel consumption: 2mpg (.71km/litre).

Range of action: 300 miles (483km).

Approach angle: 45°; departure angle, 51°.

Federal 94X43, 4 to 5 ton tractor

Typical nomenclature: truck, 4 to 5 ton, 4x4, tractor; Federal 94X43A, B, C.
Manufacturer: Federal Motor Truck Company, Detroit, Michigan.
Standard Nomenclature List: G-513.
Classification: standard.

Specification
Engine: 8,669cc Hercules RXC-529; six-cylinder water-cooled side-valve petrol engine; net power output, 112bhp at 2,200rpm; maximum torque, 395 lbf/ft at 1,000rpm.
Transmission: 5F1Rx2; over-drive top gear; part-time 4x4.
Suspension: live axles on multi-leaf semi-elliptical springs.
Brakes: air pressure; drums all-round; four trailer air-line connections.
Construction: channel-section steel ladder chassis; pressed-steel welded cab.
Electrical system: dual 6-12V.

Dimensions
Length: 17ft (5.2m). **Width,** 7ft 11in (2.4m). **Height,** (open cab, top in place) 9ft 5in (2.9m); (reduced) 7 ft 8in (2.37m).
Wheelbase: 11ft 3in (3.4m).
Ground clearance: 11.75in (30cm).
Payload: 9,350lb (4,241kg).
Weight: (unladen) 11,606lb (5,264.5kg); (gross) 21,000lb (9,525.6kg).
Normal towed load: 20,000lb (9,072kg).

Performance
Maximum allowable speed: 41mph (66kph).
Average fuel consumption: 3.5mpg (1.24km/litre).
Range of action: 180-200 miles (290-322km).
Approach angle: 54°; departure angle, 50°.

Ford/Willys Jeep, ¹/₄ ton truck

Typical nomenclature: truck, ¹/₄ ton, 4x4, cargo; Ford GPW, Willys MB.
Manufacturer: Ford Motor Company, Dearborn, Michigan. Willys-Overland Motors Inc; Toledo, Ohio.
Standard Nomenclature List: G-503.
Classification: standard.

Specification
Engine: 2,199cc Willys Go-Devil Type 441 or 442; four-cylinder water-cooled side-valve petrol engine; net power output, 54bhp at 4,000rpm; maximum torque, 105 lbf/ft at 2,000rpm.
Transmission: 3F1Rx2; part-time 4x4.
Suspension: live axles on multi-leaf semi-elliptical springs; hydraulic telescopic shock absorbers.

Right: The so-called 'Set number 7' turned a standard 1^1/$_2$ or 2^1/$_2$-ton truck into a light recovery vehicle... the US equivalent of the British breakdown gantry-type lorry. This 1^1/$_2$-ton Chevrolet carries a Jeep on suspended tow; the pulley block had a capacity of 1,100 lb (499 kg). *(PW)*

Brakes: hydraulic; drums all-round.
Construction: channel-section steel ladder chassis; pressed-steel welded body.
Electrical system: 6V.

Dimensions
Length: 11ft (3.35m). **Width,** 4ft 8in (1.4m). **Height,** (top erected) 5ft 10in (1.78m);
(reduced) 4ft 4in (1.3m).
Wheelbase: 6ft 8in (2m).
Ground clearance: 9in (23cm).
Payload: 600lb (272kg).
Weight: (unladen) 2,453lb (1,113kg); (gross) 3,253lb (1,476kg).
Normal towed load: 1,000lb (453.6kg).

Performance
Maximum allowable speed: 65mph (105kph).
Average fuel consumption: 20mpg (7.1km/litre).
Range of action: 300 miles (483km).
Approach angle: 45°; departure angle 35°.

Left: Although not in regular use on the supply routes, the 1^1/$_2$-ton Dodge WC62 6x6 (the similar WC63 was equipped with a winch) was a useful vehicle for Ordnance companies who needed to move quantities of parts or tools and equipment. More than 42,500 examples were built between 1943 and 1945. The 6x6 variant shared a large number of common parts with the more numerous ^{3}/$_4$-ton WC51 4x4 weapons carrier. *(ST)*

GMC AFKWX, 2^1/$_2$-ton truck

Typical nomenclature: truck, 2^1/$_2$-ton, 6x6, cargo, 15ft (4.6m) (or 17ft [5.2m]) body, COE; GMC AFKWX-353.
Manufacturer: GMC Truck & Coach Division, General Motors Corporation;, Pontiac, Michigan; Prior to 1943, Yellow Truck & Coach Manufacturing Company, Pontiac, Michigan.
Standard Nomenclature List: G-508, G-655.
Classification: standard.

Specification
Engine: 4,416cc GM (Chevrolet) Model 270; six-cylinder water-cooled overhead-valve petrol engine; net power output, 94bhp at 3,000rpm; maximum torque, 217 lbf/ft at 1,600rpm.
Transmission: 5F1Rx2; part-time 6x6.
Suspension: live axles on multi-leaf semi-elliptical springs.
Brakes: hydraulic with Hydrovac vacuum servo assistance; drums all-round.
Construction: channel-section steel ladder chassis; pressed-steel welded cab, welded-steel or timber body.
Electrical system: 6V.

Dimensions (long-wheelbase vehicles only)
Length: 22ft 3in (6.8m), 24ft 3in (7.4m). **Width,** 7ft 4in (2.24m). **Height,** (to top of cab) 8ft 10in (2.7m); (reduced) 7ft (2.1m).
Wheelbase: 13ft 8in (4.2m).
Bogie centres: 3ft 8in (1.12m).
Ground clearance: 10in (25cm).
Payload: 5,000lb (2,268kg).
Weight: (unladen) 10,810lb (4,093kg); (gross) 15,810lb (7,171kg).
Normal towed load: 4,500lb (2,041kg).

Performance
Maximum allowable speed: 45mph (72kph).
Average fuel consumption: 7.5mpg (2.7km/litre).
Range of action: 300 miles (483km).
Approach angle: 45°; departure angle 32.5°.

GMC CCKW, 2¹/₂-ton truck

Typical nomenclature: truck, 2¹/₂-ton, 6x6, cargo or fuel tank; GMC CCKW-352, CCKW-353.
Manufacturer: GMC Truck & Coach Division, General Motors Corporation, Pontiac, Michigan; Prior to 1943, Yellow Truck & Coach Manufacturing Company, Pontiac, Michigan.
Standard Nomenclature List: G-508.
Classification: standard.

Specification
Engine: 4,416cc GM (Chevrolet) Model 270; six-cylinder water cooled overhead-valve petrol engine; net power output, 94bhp at 3,000rpm; maximum torque, 217 lbf/ft at 1,600rpm.
Transmission: 5F1Rx2; part-time 6x6.
Suspension: live axles on multi-leaf semi-elliptical springs.
Brakes: hydraulic with Hydrovac vacuum servo assistance; drums all-round.
Construction: channel-section steel ladder chassis; pressed-steel welded cab, welded-steel or timber body.
Electrical system: 6V.

Dimensions (cargo and fuel tanker vehicles)
Length: (short-wheelbase) 19ft 2in (5.84m), (long-wheelbase) 21ft 3in (6.5m).
Width: 7ft 5in (2.3m). **Height:** (to top of cab), 9ft 2in (2.8m); (reduced), 7ft 3in (2.2m).
Wheelbase: 12ft 1in and 13ft 8in (3.7m and 4.2m) .
Bogie centres: 3ft 8in (1.12m).
Ground clearance: 10in (25cm).
Payload: (cargo vehicles) 5,000lb (2,268kg).
Capacity of fuel tanker variant: (long-wheelbase only), 2x375 gallons (2x1,425 litre).
Typical weight: (unladen) 9,635lb (4,370kg); (gross) 14,635lb (6,638kg); (fuel tanker, gross) 15,450lb (7,008kg).
Normal towed load: 4,500lb (2,041kg).

Left: Standard closed-cab 2 ¹/₂-ton GMC with all canvas in place. The presence of the spare wheels behind the cab shows that this is the short-wheelbase version (CCKW-352). The long-wheelbase version carried a single spare wheel under the chassis. *(PR)*

Above: The forward-control (cab-over-engine, or COE in US Army terms) GMC AFKWX was far less common than the normal-control CCKW but offered the advantage of having a longer truck bed. Automotive details were otherwise similar and both open and closed-cab variants were produced. *(DD)*

Right: Compare the AFWX above to the more common CCKW. *(MB)*

Performance
Maximum allowable speed: 45mph (72kph).
Average fuel consumption: 7.5mpg (2.7km/litre).
Range of action: 190 to 220 miles (306 to 354km).
Approach angle: (without winch) 54°, (with winch) 31°; departure angle (short-wheelbase) 44°, (long-wheelbase) 36°.

Harley-Davidson WLA motorcycle

Typical nomenclature: motorcycle, solo; Harley-Davidson 40-WLA, 41-WLA, 42-WLA.
Manufacturer: Harley-Davidson Motor Company, Milwaukee, Wisconsin.
Standard Nomenclature List: G523.
Classification: standard

Specification
Engine: 737cc Harley-Davidson WL; two cylinders (45° 'V'); side-valve; air-cooled petrol engine; net power output, 23bhp at 4,500rpm; torque, 28 lbf/ft at 3,000rpm.
Transmission: 3F; chain-drive to rear wheel.
Suspension: parallelogram steel tube front forks with twin coil springs; solid rear end.
Brakes: mechanical by rod and cable.
Construction: steel-tube duplex-cradle type frame.
Electrical system: 6V.

Above: The big Harley-Davidson WLA was the most numerous military motorcycle of World War Two with thousands suppplied to all of the Allies. The combination of a heavy frame, girder forks and a rugged side-valve V-twin engine was typical of US motorcycle practice of the period. Production continued into the 1950s. *(QM)*

Dimensions

Length: 7ft 4in (2.24m). Width, 3ft (.92m). **Height,** (with windshield) 5ft 1in (1.55m), (without windshield) 3ft 5in (1.04m).
Wheelbase: 4ft 10in (1.5m).
Ground clearance: 4in (10cm).
Payload: 200lb (91kg).
Weight: (unladen) 535lb (243kg); (gross) 735lb (333kg).

Performance

Maximum allowable speed: 60mph (97kph).
Average fuel consumption: 37mpg (13.1km/litre).
Range of action: 120 miles (193km).

Above: In the field repairs being carried out on a Harley-Davidson WLA. *(NA)*

Far left:
The Harley-Davidson was widely used by Military Police units, and for convoy escort and despatch rider duties. *(NA)*

IHC M425, M426, 5-ton tractor

Typical nomenclature: truck, 5 ton, 4x2, tractor, COE; M425, M426; International
Harvester H-542-9, H 542-11; Kenworth H-542-11; Marmon-Herrington H-542-11.
Manufacturer: International Harvester Company, Chicago, Illinois; Kenworth Motor Truck
Corporation, Seattle, Washington; Marmon-Herrington Company Inc, Indianapolis, Indiana.
Standard Nomenclature List: G-671.
Classification: (M425) limited standard; (M426) standard.

Specification
Engine: 7,390cc IHC Red Diamond RED-450-D; six-cylinder water-cooled overhead-
valve petrol engine; net power output, 125bhp at 2,600rpm; maximum torque, 354 lbf/ft
at 900rpm.
Transmission: 5F1R; 4x2.
Suspension: live axles on multi-leaf semi-elliptical springs; Houdaille shock absorbers.
Brakes: air pressure; drums all-round; four trailer air-line connections.
Construction: channel-section steel ladder chassis of bolted construction; pressed-steel
welded cab.
Electrical system: 6V.

Dimensions
Length: 16ft 8in (5.1m). **Width,** 8ft 1^{1}/$_{2}$in (2.5m). **Height,** (open cab, top in place)
8ft 11^{1}/$_{2}$in; (reduced) 7ft (2.7m).
Wheelbase: 10ft (3m).

Ground clearance: (M425) 9in (23cm), (M426) 10.5in (27cm).
Payload: 13,000lb (5,897kg).
Weight: (M425) (unladen) 11,400lb (5,171kg), (gross) 24,400lb (11,068kg); (M426) (unladen) 12,100lb (5,489kg), (gross) 25,100lb (11,385kg).
Normal towed load: 20,000lb (9,072kg).

Performance

Maximum allowable speed, 35-38mph (56-61kph).
Average fuel consumption, 3-4mpg (1.06-1.42km/litre).
Range of action, 240 miles (386km).
Approach angle, (M425) 32°, (M426) 35°; departure angle, (M425) 50°, (M426) 55°.

Studebaker US6, 2¹/₂-ton tractor

Typical nomenclature: truck, 2¹/₂ ton, 6x4, tractor; Studebaker US6x4-U6.
Manufacturer: Studebaker Corporation, South Bend, Indiana.
Standard Nomenclature List: G-630.
Classification: substitute standard.

Specification

Engine: 5,245cc Hercules JXD; six-cylinder water-cooled side-valve petrol engine; net power output, 87bhp at 2,600rpm; maximum torque, 238 lbf/ft at 1,100rpm.
Transmission: 5F1R (5F1Rx2 on late production); over-drive top gear; 6x4.
Suspension: live axles on multi-leaf semi-elliptical springs, inverted at rear.

Above: GMC was only one of the US companies manufacturing 2¹/₂-ton trucks; others were built by International and Studebaker. The Studebaker US6 was similar in appearance to the GMC and was constructed in cargo, tanker, side and rear tipper, and tractor form. As with the GMC, there were also open and closed-cab variants. *(DD)*

Above: Studebaker US6 tractor for semi-trailer. *(DD)*

Brakes: hydraulic, with vacuum servo assistance; drums all-round; electric connection for trailer brakes.
Construction: channel-section steel ladder chassis; pressed-steel welded cab.
Electrical system: 6V.

Dimensions (tractor variant only)
Length: 18ft 1in (5.5m). **Width,** 7ft 3in (2.2m). **Height,** (closed cab) 7ft 3in (2.2m).
Wheelbase: 12ft 4in (3.8m).
Ground clearance: 10in (25cm).
Payload: 15,650lb (7,099kg).
Weight: (unladen) 8,190lb (3,715kg); (gross) 23,840lb (10,814kg).
Normal towed load: 21,000lb (9,526kg).

Performance
Maximum allowable speed: 45mph (72kph).
Average fuel consumption: 8mpg (2.8km/litre).
Range of action: 320 miles (515km).
Approach angle: 52°; departure angle, 45°.

Ward LaFrance Model 1000, 6-ton wrecker

Typical nomenclature: truck, wrecking, heavy, M1A1; Ward LaFrance Model 1000 Series 5, Kenworth Model 573.
Manufacturer: Kenworth Motor Truck Corporation, Seattle, Washington; Ward LaFrance Truck Corporation, Division of Great American Industries Inc, Elmira, New York.

Standard Nomenclature List: G-116.
Classification: standard.

Specification

Engine: 8,210cc Continental 22R; six-cylinder water-cooled overhead-valve petrol engine; net power output, 133bhp at 2,400rpm; maximum torque, 372 lbf/ft at 1,200rpm.
Transmission: 5F1Rx2; part-time 6x6.
Suspension: live axles on multi-leaf semi-elliptical springs; inverted at rear; hydraulic shock absorbers at front.
Brakes: air-pressure operated; brake line connections at front and rear for towing.
Construction: steel ladder chassis; pressed-steel welded cab and body.
Electrical system: 12V.

Dimensions

Length: 29ft (8.8m). **Width,** 8ft 4in (2.5m). **Height,** 10ft (3m).
Wheelbase: 15ft 1in (4.6m).
Bogie centres: 4ft 4in (1.3m).
Ground clearance: 12.75in (32cm).
Weight: (unladen) 27,330lb (12,397kg), (gross) 35,330lb (16,026kg).
Maximum towed load: 60,000lb (27,216kg).

Performance

Maximum allowable speed: 45mph (72kph).
Average fuel consumption: 2.5mpg (.9kp/litre).
Range of action: 250 miles (402km).
Approach angle: 55°; departure angle, 55°.

Above: The standardised M1A1 heavy wrecker was produced by Kenworth and Ward LaFrance; the two machines were identical in almost every detail. The wrecking gear was a single-boom type supplied by Gar Wood. *(PW)*

Above: Corbitt and GMC trucks await loading at a beach-head depot after the D-Day landings, 6 June 1944. *(PW)*